Anonymous

The Pilgrim with the Ancient Book

and other sacred poems

Anonymous

The Pilgrim with the Ancient Book
and other sacred poems

ISBN/EAN: 9783337295035

Printed in Europe, USA, Canada, Australia, Japan

Cover: Foto ©Lupo / pixelio.de

More available books at **www.hansebooks.com**

THE PILGRIM

WITH

THE ANCIENT BOOK.

AND

OTHER SACRED POEMS.

BY

M. N. C.

LONDON:
WILLIAM HUNT AND COMPANY,
23, Holles Street, Cavendish Square,
BATH: G. SHORT, MILSOM STREET.

1868.

Dedication.

To all who love

THE LORD JESUS CHRIST,

this little

VOLUME OF SACRED SONG

IS DEDICATED,

"*In simplicity and Godly sincerity by the Grace of God,*"

by

THE AUTHOR.

Scripture Mottos.

MATTHEW XXV. 15.   MARK XIII. 34.

"And to another one; to every man according to his several ability." "And to every man his work."

ROMANS XII. 6.   I CORINTHIANS VII. 7; XII. 4, 11.

"Having then gifts differing according to the grace that is given to us." "Every man hath his proper gift." "There are diversities of gifts, but the same spirit." "The selfsame Spirit, dividing to every man severally as He will."

EPHESIANS V. 19.   COLOSSIANS III. 16.

"Be filled with the Spirit; speaking to yourselves in psalms and hymns and spiritual songs, singing and making melody in your heart to the Lord." "Let the word of Christ dwell in you richly in all wisdom; teaching and admonishing one another in psalms and hymns and spiritual songs, singing with grace in your hearts to the Lord."

I CORINTHIANS XIV. 15.

"I will sing with the spirit, and I will sing with the understanding also."

PSALM IX. 2.   *(Prayer Book version.)*

"Yea, my songs will I make of Thy Name, O Thou most Highest."

Contents.

	Page
The Pilgrim with the Ancient Book	1
The Pilgrim with the Ancient Book (Part ii.)	8
Prayer	13
Our Lord's Prayer	17
Shew me Thy Glory	18
I will Praise the Name of God	20
His Name shall be called Wonderful	23
Jesus Christ of Nazareth	26
The Name of the Lord	29
I will love Thee, O Lord!	32
Thou art my God	35
Thou art my Praise	37
Adoration	39
The Sons of God	41
Praise	42
The Eagle-Flight	44
The Dove and the Ark	47

CONTENTS.

	Page
Peace and Love	48
Thy Word	49
Where art Thou?	52
Glorious Liberty	54
A Spiritual Song and Psalm of Life	56
No Cross! No Crown!!	61
He restoreth my soul	62
Submission	65
Be Vigilant	66
A Sacred Poem	67
Yesterday, and To-day, and for Ever	71
Wonderful	73
Bought with a Price	74
Issues of Life	75
A Spiritual Song	78
God Manifest in the Flesh	79
A Dialogue	82
A Hymn	83
Sing, O ye Heavens	85
Tears	86
Wrath of the Lamb. The Terror of the Lord	88
Blood of the Lamb	90
The Hiding Place	92
Heart Communings	94
A Broken Heart, O God!	96
Balm of Gilead	97

CONTENTS.

	Page
The Fruits of the Spirit	99
A Lamb as it had been Slain	100
A Spiritul Ode	102
The Great Brother!	104
Who loved Me	106
A Song of Zion	108
The Power of Christ	110
The City of God	112
Living Bread	114
The Mount of God	116
A Spiritual Song	117
A Contrast	119
Repentance to Salvation	121
He Careth for You	123
Glory in the Lord	125
Leaning upon Her Beloved	127
Awake!	129
A little lower than the Angels	131
Is it True?	133
Hide Me	134
Ambition	136
One Word	139
The Three Marys	140
The Ministry of Angels	141
A Hymn	143
Eye hath not seen	144

CONTENTS.

	Page
Glorious Liberty	145
Jehovah Nissi	147
A Spiritual Battle Song, for a Good Soldier of Jesus Christ	150
The Reconciling Tree	152
The Armies in Heaven	154
Honouroble Marriage	157
Christ our Life	160
The Blood of Jesus Christ	161
The Lord my Salvation	163
A Protestant Layman's Catholic Confession	164
Awake, awake, put on strength, O arm of the Lord!	165
A Protestant Ballad of the Nineteenth Century	167
He is the Rock	170
The Harps of God	174
The Church of God	176
A Lutheran Epigram	178
A Romish Epigram	178
Vox Populi	178
A Sinner Saved by Grace	179

The Pilgrim with the Ancient Book.

"HOMO UNIUS LIBRI."

Eccl. xii. 12.   Jer. xv. 16.   John xxi. 25.

E was a man of only one small Book,
Most other reading he had long forsook;
His single aim he noiselessly pursued,
Whereby much peace and wisdom had accrued.

Of making many books there was no end,
Which did, he said, to sore distraction tend;
Much study was a weariness to flesh,
But God's sweet Book was ever new and fresh.

While vain philosophers would fain be wise,
Crude shallow science God's deep truth denies;
Its holy wisdom, sparkling thoughts divine,
Made glad the heart, as with old mellow wine.

It taught the science of the new creation,
Its ancient, everlasting, firm foundation
In the great Rock of Ages deeply laid,
Ere the young mountains of the earth were made.

THE PILGRIM WITH THE ANCIENT BOOK.

It was all histories in one combin'd,—
The present, past, and future of mankind;
Bright rays and beams from each prophetic page
Shed their effulgence over every age.

His chief companion was this little Book,
Wherein he oftentimes was wont to look:
He said, it was in every page and part
The joy and deep rejoicing of his heart.

Its precepts he had pondered from his youth,
And found them ever full of old, new truth;
Than droppings of the honey-comb more sweet,
With never-cloying richness still replete.

Thousands of gold and silver could not buy
The hidden treasure that in it did lie;—
It was a rich and most productive mine,
Wherein he found rare costly gems divine.

It told him of one tried and precious stone,
By most philosophers unsought, unknown,—
By faith's alchemic touch it turned to gold,
Whate'er in contact with it you might hold.

And this was its recorded certain token,—
Who stumbled o'er it should be sorely broken;
But upon whomsoever it should fall,
'Twould grind to powder, whether great or small.

THE PILGRIM WITH THE ANCIENT BOOK.

He called his Book a lamp unto his feet,
To guide him through this dark world's crooked street;
A light to show the pathway day by day,
Lest in his journey he should lose his way.

He was a sojourner and stranger here,
But so, he said, that all his fathers were;
They all were pilgrims,—and he mentioned some
Who'd gone before, and they all bade him come.

It was the oldest and most proven Book,
Whose deep foundations never could be shook;
It learned him more than all the ancients knew,—
It was "The Word of GOD," and GOD was True.

The secret of its proof was hid within;
Nor could the senseless dogmatistic din
Of seven-fold heresy, disturb the voice
Which bade the spirit-depths, "Be still: rejoice!"

Cavils and carpings made it more secure;
It could and must for ever stand, endure:
Wild waves, that madly dash against a rock,
Are spent in foam, recoiling from the shock.

Prophets, Apostles, Sages, old and young,
Its truths and triumphs evermore have sung;
Science and history alike unfold
Th' ancient and modern miracles foretold.

THE PILGRIM WITH THE ANCIENT BOOK.

This was a Book, he said, to make one wise, —
Its light most pleasant to meek lowly eyes;
But burning flames could rise to scorch and blind
The lofty look, the proud and haughty mind.

He called it too a secret magic Book,
A burnished mirror, wherein he could look;
Whose inward glory was so bright and strange,
That all his features seemed to shine and change.

Again,—he called it a two-edgèd sword,
Which once was wielded by his Captain-Lord;
Clothed with the strength and armour of his God,
Calmly, courageously his course he trod.

That armour had been proved in many a field,
Helmet and corselet, greaves, and well-tried shield:
The noble army of the martyr-host
All gained the day ere they gave up the ghost.

Right many foes full well he knew he had,
But to retreat his orders all forbad;
In danger too, his Captain would draw near,
Deliver him from all his foes and fear.

At times, he owned, Doubt whispered, then withdrew
The peace and calmness that his spirit knew;
Then was the time to pray, and soon again
Brave Faith returned, with his Fair Sisters twain.

THE PILGRIM WITH THE ANCIENT BOOK.

He said that sometimes as he conned his Book,
'Twas as if strolling by some cool clear brook,
Whose quiet waters gently gliding by
Filled all his soul with tranquil ecstacy :

Or, resting in fair fields of tender grass,
Soft zephyrs o'er his grateful brow should pass,
Breathing sweet odours as of many flowers,
Such as might bloom in amaranthine bowers.

And should "the High and Lofty One," on high
Inhabiting the vast eternity !
Vouchsafe to visit his unworthy breast,
That moment might not be by words exprest :
Entrancingly unutterably blest !

Oh how he did this ancient Book revere !
It taught him whom to honour, love, or fear ;
Its words were full of spirit and of life,
With holy wit and wisdom teeming, rife :

The words of One who spake as ne'er before
Man ever spake, nor shall speak evermore :
It was his meditation all the day,
And some choice portions he by heart could say.

That meditation was so rich and sweet,
As though all harmonies in one should meet,
And fall upon th' entranced enraptured spirit,
With melody celestial charm and fill it.

THE PILGRIM WITH THE ANCIENT BOOK.

" The Lord his Shepherd was: he could not want!
(His soul should make her boast, and meekly vaunt)
His Sun and Shield! and He would freely give
Both grace and glory, and his heart should live!"

When prone, alas! to stumble, slip, or fall,
In tender tones of kind rebuke He'd call,—
Restore his soul, and lead him in the way
Of righteousness, from which his feet would stray.

Still be believed that to his journey's end
His Shepherd's grace and goodness would extend;
Then in His home for ever he should dwell,
His matchless love and praise for ever tell:

The many-mansioned house and home above,
Where the great Father dwelt in cloudless love,
And where the Shepherd still prepares a place
For every pilgrim who receives His grace.

His Lord and Master had the noblest Name,
His glory was so great,—'twas past all fame;
At all times he would bless and praise his Lord,
Who such sweet loving kindness did afford.

The Church, he said, was built upon a Rock,
Calmly she met each hell-conspired shock;
By God Himself her sure foundation laid
In Christ Himself,—as Paul and Peter said.

THE PILGRIM WITH THE ANCIENT BOOK.

She raised her lofty brow to heaven on *high*,
Her lowly heart stooped *low* as sinners lie,
Her arms outwide she stretched, as *broad* and *free*
As west from east, o'er every land and sea.

Her great High-Priest and Head now ruled above,
As every child by faith and prayer might prove;
And He in glory soon would come again,
With all His saints, triumphantly to reign.

Each faithful pilgrim was both priest and saint,
Undecked with sacerdotal garb or paint;
In the true calendar enrolled above,—
The Lamb's great Book of life, and grace, and love.

The Pilgrim with the Ancient Book.

PART II.

1 Timothy iii. 16.

THIS pilgrim read me how that once his God
A pilgrim was, and the same path had trod;
His Lord and God as man was once disguised,
By man rejected, set at nought, despised.

He came enrobed in meekness from above,
To teach mankind both Law and Gospel love;
He came unto His own: but oh! foul blot,
Ungratefully His own received Him not.

He read of His Divine, yet lowly birth,
Which filled the angels with deep wondering mirth,
As their glad hymns so blithesomely they sang,
The azure welkin with the anthem rang:—

"Glory to God, on high! good will to man!"
The old and new eternal gracious plan,—
Mercy and Truth, Peace, Righteousness, and Love,
Have now come down to earth from heaven above.

THE PILGRIM WITH THE ANCIENT BOOK.

But far the strangest tale of all was when
(Blasphemed, and mocked, and scourged by cruel men)
They led Him up, towards "the mournful hill,"
Mid savage scorn,—to crucify and kill.

And there they slew Him : there his Lord had died!
While a fierce soldier pierced His blessed side :
From heart and thorn-crowned brow, from hands and feet,
Welled forth the stream Divine, with life replete,

Of crimson blood, and crystal water clear,—
To wash out man's red guilt and shame and fear ;
To heal the broken heart, its grief control,
And to make white as snow each tainted soul.

A rich man laid Him in his own new grave,—
The Lord ! who came both poor and rich to save ;
While loving women, with tear-sprinkled care,
Spices and ointments to embalm prepare.

'Tis vain : He needs it not ! He rose again :
The tomb and temple's veil both rent in twain !
In His own might He rose, and burst the prison.
Angels announce with joy,—"The Lord is risen."

The pilgrim said,—if all his Lord had done
His wondrous acts were written every one,
They never could (as he supposed) be told ;
The world itself the volumes would not hold.[b]

THE PILGRIM WITH THE ANCIENT BOOK.

Veiled in His manhood all the Godhead dwelt,
Who in Gethsemane's sad garden knelt,—
Bore on the cross the weight of all our woe,
And bruised the head of God and man's great foe.

Yet He could stoop the little ones to bless,
And take them up with gracious gentleness;
If Jesus ever smiled, perchance 'twas when
Babes smiling met His kind-eyed loving ken.

"A Man of Sorrows, and acquaint with grief,"
His peaceful moments were both rare and brief;
Oft-times He'd wend in solitude His way
To mountain's top or garden's shade to pray.

The servant was not greater than his Lord:
To Him this world did not much gain afford;—
No place of rest to lay His gracious Head,
Who multitudes with miracles oft fed.

A sick one crept to touch His seamless robe;
Such was the virtue in its hem to probe
The secret source of long acute disease,
That instantaneous was the blest release.

And once a sad one, as He sat at meat,
Knelt and embraced His holy sacred feet,
Washed them with flowing tears, and then with care
She dried them with her wild luxuriant hair.

THE PILGRIM WITH THE ANCIENT BOOK.

Again she came,—but now with precious ointment:
Moved with deep love, and by Divine appointment,
This time she gently pours it o'er His head,
For all her sins, and fears, and tears are fled.

At Sychar's well, when weary, worn, and sad,
To that strange woman who five husbands had,
Strange words He spake, which made her wondering think,—
Drew the deep living water,—bade her drink.

They tell Him of a dark, foul, mournful fact.
"What sayest thou?" "One taken in the act.
Such Moses hath commanded us to stone."—
"Who hath no sin, by him the first be thrown."

They went out, one by one. She stands alone:—
"Whither are thine accusers, woman, gone?
Hath none condemned, of all who stood before?
Neither do I condemn: Go: sin no more."

He loved His own, and loved them to the end,—
No faithlessness in that unchanging Friend;
Through sad denial, dark desertion, shame,
More brightly glowed the self-consuming flame.

Myself,—I love to meditate and dwell
On all that this meek pilgrim had to tell;
"The wondrous things" and words of that blest Book,
In which, he said, the angels longed to look.

THE PILGRIM WITH THE ANCIENT BOOK.

The mystery for ages long concealed,
Now to the favoured sons of men revealed;
God manifested in the flesh, made known
In Him, in whom the Father's glory shone.

My sister, brother, hast thou read my song,
Followed my pilgrim's simple tale along?
Like him may we both daily search and look
Into this ancient, true, and holy Book:

With child-like wisdom, God-like faith believe
The grandest truth man's spirit can receive:
So childish reasonings and doubts shall melt
As night-bred mists when morn's bright beams are felt.

So may we reach at last the heavenly shore
As our brave Pilgrim Fathers have before;
Who now from all their toil and labour rest
In our great Father's house for ever blest.

The way is Christ, the Spirit hath declared,
Who once our pilgrimage and sorrow shared;
Led by that Spirit in the path He trod,
We are joint heirs with Him, and sons of God!^c

^a 2 Cor. iii. 18; iv. 6.
^b John xxi. 25.
^c Rom. viii. 17.

Prayer.

JAMES V. 15—18.

 SING the wonders prayer hath wrought,—
    Its universal power and fame,
When, by the Holy Spirit taught,
    Saints call upon Jehovah's name!

" The prayer of faith" rules heaven and earth,
    And moves the mighty God of Love,—
Now brings the devastating dearth,
    Now "showers of blessings" from above.

Prayer wields the ancient Prophet's rod; [a]
    Angels and elements obey:
It *moves* the chariot wheels of God,
    When men of prayer in earnest pray.

When God's High Priest bowed down, and prayed
    Between the living and the dead, [b]
The soul-destroying plague was stayed,
    Which fiercely through the camp had spread.

PRAYER.

"It shall not rain," Elijah says;^c
   Lo, drought and famine, sun-scorched years:
"Seven times" the prophet bends and prays;
   Behold! the little cloud appears!

"The man of God" to Judah's king ^d
   Proclaims dread summons from on high:
"Monarch! a message stern I bring,—
   Arrange thy home, for thou must die."

The smitten king in anguish cries,
   Weeps sore, with bitter flowing tears;
Again Jehovah's word replies,—
   "Lo, I have added fifteen years."

The prophet-prince is bowed with grief,^e
   In deep humiliation bent;
An angel flies to his relief,
   By the great King of angels sent.

Peter lies bound with doubled chains, ^f
   Most vigilantly watched and kept,
Throughout his cell deep silence reigns,
   As calmly he reposed and slept.

But, hark! incessant prayer ascends
   From yon small chamber, night and day:
Again the King His angel sends,
   And frees the prisoner while they pray.

PRAYER.

The Prince and Priest of all our race
    Was wont to pass whole nights in prayer,—
Would oft to some secluded place
    In secrecy unseen repair.

To righteous men still, still avails
    Th' effectual fervent earnest prayer;
Wrestling with Jacob's God prevails,
    Whose angels hover everywhere.

True prayer is God's own voice within
    The Christian's groaning heart and breast;
The Spirit battling with our sin,
    Wrestling, and giving God no rest.

" Until Thou bless, Thou shalt not go;
    I will not loose my hold on Thee;
Loose Thou my bonds, then shall I know
    My God Himself hath set me free!"

Let prayer and praise join hand in hand,
    Ascend before Jehovah's face;
Behold the Intercessor stand—[g]
    Yield to the Spirit's pleading grace.

In Jesu's all-prevailing name,[h]
    The Father's love hath so decreed,
The prayer of faith is still the same,
    And must triumphantly succeed.

PRAYER.

In every clime, in every age,
   The wondrous works of God declare,—
The sacred, and the historic page,
   The glories of potential prayer.

NOTES.

^a "Take Moses' rod, the rod of prayer."—*Christian Year*, "Easter Eve."

^b Numbers xvi. 46—48.

^c 1 Kings xvii. 1 ; xviii. 42—45.

^d 2 Kings xx. 1—5.

^e Daniel ix. 20—23.

^f Acts xii. 6—17.

^g Rom. viii. 26, 27, 34 ; Heb. ii. 17, 18 ; iv. 11—16 ; vii. 24—27.

^h John xiv. 13, 14 ; xvi. 23, 24.

Our Lord's Prayer.
A PARAPHRASE.

REAT Father! of our ransomed race,
Enthroned in heaven's high holy place!
Whose Holy, Holy, Holy Name
Is everlastingly the same:
Thrice hallowed be Thy Triune fame!
Thine, and Thy dear Son's kingdom come,
All this world's kingdoms His become;[a]
Thy heavenly will on earth be done,
In every clime beneath the sun:
Oh! give Thy children day by day
The bread, and blessed grace that may
Both soul and body nourish, feed;
Give heav'nly meat and drink indeed:
Our trespasses, our debts forgive,
To Christ indebted now to live;
For His dear sake henceforth may we
Our brother-debtors loose and free:
Oh, lead not into trial's fire,
Temptation subtle, deep or dire;
But from the Evil One defend,—
Deliver, rescue to the end.
Thine is the kingdom, glory, power,
In heaven or earth, each day, each hour:
In height above, in depth beneath,
Let every living thing with breath
To Thee, the living Father, raise
An endless anthem, psalm of praise,—
Sing, with the heavenly seraph-host,
To Father, Son, and Holy Ghost!

[a] Rev. xi. 15—17.

"Shew me Thy Glory."

"I beseech Thee, shew me Thy glory."
Exodus xxxiii. 18.

"Thou hast made me exceeding glad with Thy countenance."
Psalm xxi. 6.

"And His countenance as the sun shineth in his strength."
Revelation i. 16.

"One smile from JEHOVAH'S *countenance."*
Rev. J. Hamilton's B. D.
Lessons from the Gt. Biography, p. 6.

SHEW me Thy glory, I beseech Thee, Lord!
   One smile from Thy bright countenance Divine,
Soul-satiating gladness shall afford,
   And make my heart with holy joy to shine.

As in a mirror of pure burnished gold,
   Express reflection of the Father's grace,
JEHOVAH'S glory man may now behold—
   Yet *unconsumed,*—in Christ's immortal face.

O soul-revealing vision! glory-glance!
   When by the Spirit's light the depths within
Are pierced; and viewed, as in prophetic trance,[a]
   "Chambers of imagery" foul with sin;

"SHEW ME THY GLORY."

"All forms of creeping things," corrupt and vile,
  "Abominations" desperately base,
The temple of the soul despoil, defile;
  God's image desecrate, destroy, disgrace.

But O the glory of the new creation!
  Complete and perfect in the risen Lord,—
As, by the Spirit's blest irradiation,
  The fane is now rebuilt, regilt, restor'd.

O glory-glance! O soul-enchanting vision!
  Sweet smile from that bright countenance Divine—
The God of this world's blinded fools' derision [b]—
  Yet more transformingly within me shine.

That I, with confidential holy fear,
  May stand and gaze unveiled, and live for ever;
As to the true SHEKINAH I draw near,
  From Whom henceforth no cloud may hide or sever.

Lo! Glory, Wisdom, Light and Love, combining
  The everlasting God's evangel-grace;
The fulness of the Triune GODHEAD shining
  In JESUS' many-crowned [c] exalted face!

[a] Ezek. viii.   [b] 2 Cor. iv. 4, 6.   [c] Rev. xix. 11—16.

"I will Praise the Name of God."

"*I will praise the name of God with a song, and will magnify Him with thanksgiving.*"

Psalm lxix. 30, 31.

....."*Yea, my songs will I make of Thy name, O Thou Most Highest.*"

Psalm ix. 2. (P. B. ver.)

ES! I would sing that great and glorious Name,
    Which angels love in loftiest hymns to praise;
My grateful soul her part would humbly claim,
    Her tribute meek of adoration raise.

No mortal pen may e'er exhaust the theme,
    The mystery for ages long concealed;
The lost from death and ruin to redeem,
    "The Son of God," as "Son of Man," revealed.

Eternal Wisdom, Justice, Mercy blent,
    Grace, Goodness, Might, and Gentleness combin'd;
The glorious message from on high was sent,
    That Love had found a ransom for mankind.

"I WILL PRAISE THE NAME OF GOD."

Jesus! Emmanuel, Jehovah known;
   "God in the flesh made manifest" to man:
The powers of death and darkness overthrown,
   The curse destroyed,—sin's just yet awful ban.

An everlasting righteousness brought in,
   Eternal life and glory freely given,
Paid the tremendous wages of our sin,
   Purchased the bright inheritance of heaven.

Slain the one all-atoning Sacrifice,—
   The "Spotless Lamb," before all worlds ordained;
Shed the all-cleansing blood of richest price,
   To heal the soul with sin's infection stained.

Lo! upward gaze! Behold at God's right hand,
   By His own blood for ever entered in,
Our Great High Priest exalted takes His stand,
   "An Advocate" who only pleads to win!

Yet forward gaze! He comes, He comes again!
   "Lift up your heads, ye everlasting gates!"
"Who comes?" "The King of Glory" comes to reign:
   The joyous advent His fair Bride awaits.

He comes on clouds majestically seated,
   Armies of angels wheeling round His throne;
The old usurper now cast out, defeated,
   The kingdoms of this world become His own.

"I WILL PRAISE THE NAME OF GOD."

Shout, Zion, shout! Thy King returns again!
    Awake, O Israël, from slumber, wake!
Go forth, go forth, thy Passover is slain,
    Thy desolate, thy long-lost land retake!

Be still, ye nations! Earth, thy silence keep!
    The Lord ariseth from His throne on high;
Ye saints, ye sons of God, no longer weep,
    "Lift up your heads: redemption draweth nigh!"

Redemption, long expected, comes at last,
    Creation's groans and travail soon shall cease;
Ere long the closing pangs and throes be past,
    That usher in the birth of endless peace.

"His Name shall be called Wonderful."

ISAIAH IX. 6.

WONDERFUL and wonder-working Name!
May mortal pen Thy majesty proclaim?
Redeemed from bondage, sin, and death, and
    hell,
Thy matchless love to all I fain would tell.

To Thy loved Name, dear Lord, I'd frame my song,
To whom compassions, mercies rich belong;
With glad thanksgivings I would fill my lay,
And bless and magnify Thee all the day.

In the night season I would ofttimes raise
A song of joyful gratitude and praise;
At midnight^a would arise Thy love to sing,
At morning light a free-will offering bring.

O "Jesus Christ of Nazareth!" Thy Name
Of old wrought wonders, and is still the same;
'Tis wonderful through faith man's soul to save,
To win the blessings that in prayer we crave.

"HIS NAME SHALL BE

'Tis wonderful in every time of need
Before "the throne of grace" thy Name to plead;
Thou, Great High Priest, art merciful on high,
And faithful, who Thyself canst not deny.

O wondrous Sacrifice! O worthy Lamb!
Worthy to stand before the Great "I AM:"
Equal with God, and yet most perfect Man,
Alpha, Omega of salvation's plan!

All power in heaven, on earth, to Thee belongs,
'Tis Thine to rectify Thy people's wrongs;
Who trust in Thee shall never be dismay'd,
What though Thy promise seem awhile delay'd.

Ah! who may all Thy noble acts express?
Who, loving-kindness, judgment, righteousness,[b]
Delight'st in all the earth to bring to pass,
As sin-blind dreamers' feeble thoughts surpass.

Boast not, vain man, thine erring reason's light!
Boast not, O mighty man, thy fragile might!
O Dives, boast not of thy golden store,—
The Lord both maketh rich and maketh poor!

He bringeth down the mighty from their seat,
Taketh the crafty in his own conceit;
His own right hand, His wisdom, counsel, thought,
Shall cause to come to pass, or come to nought.[c]

CALLED WONDERFUL."

But who may tell the wonders of His Name,
And all its glorious majesty proclaim?
Too vast, too grand the theme for mortal pen,
And raised above the loftiest angel's ken.

Yet would my soul exalt the Name ador'd,
And make her boast, and glory in the Lord;
And all within unite my God to bless,—
Rock of my wisdom, strength, peace, righteousness.

[a] Psalm xlii. 8; cxix. 62.

[b] Jer. ix. 23, 24.   [c] Lam. iii. 37.

"Jesus Christ of Nazareth."

ACTS III. 6; IV. 10—12.

ESUS CHRIST of Nazareth! What spell is in that Name
To heal the blind, the deaf, the dumb, the maimèd, halt, and lame;
To soothe the troubled conscience and the sin-tormented soul,
And e'en the fierce assaults of hell and devils to control:
O wonderful almighty Name! O everlasting Word!
"Emmanuel," our God with us! Jehovah, Christ the Lord!
Name nobler far than every name in earth or heaven above,
Alpha, Omega, First and Last, Eternal Life and Love!
Sun! whose ten thousand brilliant beams and glorious rays dispel
Tempest and storms, and blackest clouds of sin and death and hell;
Shield! to defend from fiercest dart of soul-assaulting foe:
Balm! of most wondrous power to soothe each agonizing throe;
Physician! whose almighty skill no sickness e'er can foil,
Who sleepeth neither day nor night, nor spareth care nor toil;

"JESUS CHRIST OF NAZARETH."

Shepherd! whose own right hand His flock doth feed and guard and keep;
Door of the Fold! through which alone can enter in the sheep;
Pearl of rare price! whose value yet by angels ne'er was told,
Compared to which e'en less than dross were countless mines of gold;
Castle of Hope, and Fort of Faith! Bower of peace and rest
To souls of sinners wounded sore, most grievously opprest:
Rock of Eternity! on which eternally shall stand
The glorious fabric of Thy Church, built by Thine own right hand;
Fountain of Living Waters, and Bread of Endless Life!
Omnipotent! by word to calm wild elemental strife,
Omnipotent! to walk upon the storm-uplifted wave,
Omnipotent! of sinners chief to th' uttermost to save.
The Lion bold of Judah's tribe, of David branch and root!
At once the True and Living Vine! its juice, and sap, and fruit;
The Prince of Peace, the Lord of Life, Beginning and the End!
The Everlasting Father, and the true unchanging Friend,
Great King of kings, and Lord of lords, the Lamb for sinners slain!
High Priest! who now to intercede doth ever live and reign;

"JESUS CHRIST OF NAZARETH."

Daysman![a] betwixt a sin-stained world and sin-abhorring God,
Who from His own pure veins outpoured the rich sin-cleansing blood;
By Whom, on God's own altar *once* was expiation made,
On Whom, the law's dread curse and all our guilt and shame were laid;
To Whom, from all above, below, redeemed in earth and heaven,
Glory and everlasting praise eternally be given;
Let all creation cry aloud! Let universe upraise
To Father, Son, and Holy Ghost, an endless peal of praise!

[a] Job ix. 33.

"The Name of the Lord."

"The name of the Lord is a strong tower: the righteous runneth into it, and is safe." *

Proverbs xviii. 10.

THE name of Jesus is a tower of strength,
   Built on the lofty rock of God's free grace;
   Thither the righteous runneth, and at length
   Findeth a shelter and safe hiding-place,
Where "the old serpent" may not enter in,
Nor any of the brood of soul-tormenting sin.

From its high turret calmly gazing round,
   In the bright armour of his God equipp'd,
"The fiery darts" that thickly strew the ground,
   In hell's own poison though they once were dipp'd,
He views with awe, a hissing crackling heap,
And "the old dragon" midst them sorely wounded creep.

With loud exulting shout he hails afar
   His comrades toiling in the deadly strife:
Bids them "look up," points to that wondrous Star,
   Serenely shining o'er the path of life,

* ("is set aloft."—Margin.)

THE NAME OF THE LORD.

Whose ray can penetrate the darkest gloom,
And gild with light and joy the dying hero's tomb.

A goodly banner from that turret waves
   Its crimson folds the warrior's head above,
Emblazoned with His glorious name who saves
   By His own blood, His righteousness, His love;
His own right hand and holy arm alone,
The powers of darkness, death, and hell have overthrown.

Soldiers of Jesus Christ, march boldly on!
   Steadfast and true, and "faithful unto death;"
A countless multitude have nobly won,[a]
   And shouted "victory!" with dying breath:
From every kindred, nation, tongue, and tribe,
Who to the Lamb of God salvation now ascribe.

Their robes they've washed in His most precious blood,
   And made them whiter than the purest snow;
Onward they pressed, through dangers, fire, and flood,
   Through the "much tribulation" all must know;
And now of kings and priests a bright-robed band
Before the throne of God, both day and night they stand.[b]

No biting hunger, parching thirst again,
   No sun may light on them with ardent ray,
No curse, no death, no sorrow, no more pain,
   "For all the former things are passed away;"

THE NAME OF THE LORD.

And He who sits upon the eternal throne,
Shall ever dwell among them, and their God be known.

The Lamb Himself the happy flock shall lead
   To living springs of water, cool and clear,
In heavenly fields to roam, or rest, and feed;
   From every eye shall God wipe every tear,
And all around, within, beneath, above,
An atmosphere of everlasting light, life, love!

<blockquote>
ª See Rev. vii. 9—17.

ᵇ See Rev. vii. 9—17, and xxi. 3, 4.
</blockquote>

"I will love Thee, O Lord!"

PSALM XVIII. 1.

ESUS, Lord of heaven and earth,
    Thy great Name I'd sing;
View Thee from Thine infant birth,
    Shepherd, Saviour, King!

From the cradle to the grave
    All Thy life was love:
Man's immortal soul to save
    Brought Thee from above.

Pain and anguish from the womb,
    Sorrows, trials, woes,
All pursued Thee to the tomb,
    All for our repose.

Every trait of Thy blest life
    Beamed with love benign,
With compassions countless rife,
    Philanthropy Divine.

"I WILL LOVE THEE, O LORD!"

In Thy boyhood wisdom shone
    Forth with radiance clear,
Pharisees and Scribes must own,—
    All who come to hear.

All to do Thy Father's will,
    Through distress severe,
All His purpose to fulfil,
    Thy sad, stern career.

Onward through the toil and strife,—
    Satan, death, and hell,
Leagued to overthrow Thy life,
    Vain their cursèd spell.

Thou hast triumphed, Thou hast won,
    Righteousness hast done,
God's own true and noble Son!
    God and Man in one!

All the holy law obeyed
    In Thy spotless life,
All its curse on Thee was laid,
    In Thy death's dread strife.

All temptation's force was hurl'd
    Thee to overthrow;
Thou hast overcome the world,
    And our mortal foe.

"*I WILL LOVE THEE, O LORD!*"

All the devil's work destroy'd,
  Ta'en away our sin,
Condemnation's null and void,
  Grace has entered in.

Grace and truth in Christ have met,
  Righteousness and peace ;
O the everlasting debt,
  O the blest release !

Jesus lived, and Jesus died,
  Jesus rose again !
Jesus Christ was crucified,
  Jesus Christ doth reign !

He,—" The Lamb of God," was slain,
  His pure blood was shed !
By His life we live again,
  In His death we're dead.

Let us all to Him ascribe
  Free salvation's fame ;
Every nation, tongue, and tribe,
  Laud his glorious Name !

"Thou art my God."

PSALM XXXI. 14.

"Thou art my God! Let me again repeat the glorious accents, and hear the pleasurable sounds; let me a thousand and a thousand times repeat it, it is rapture all and harmony: the harps of angels and their tongues, what notes more melodious could they sing or play? What but these transporting words give their emphasis to all their joys? On this they dwell, it is their eternal theme,—'Thou art my God!' Like me, every seraph boasts the glorious property, and owes his happiness to those important words: in them unbounded joys are comprehended. Paradise itself, all heaven, is here described; all that is possible to be uttered of celestial blessedness is here contained."—BP. HALL.

"THOU art my God!" to whom else can I go?
From Thee the streams of life eternal flow:
There's nought on earth, there's nought in heaven above
Compared to Thee! and Thy transcendent love!

"Thou art my God!" what soul-entrancing sound!
To cause the heart with holiest joy to bound,
To fill the spirit's inmost depths with light,
And yield an ever-new and strange delight.

"THOU ART MY GOD."

E'en loftiest Seraph knows no richer bliss,
For heaven itself is all comprised in this:
"Thou art my God!" Thou fount of endless love,
My peace below, my longed-for rest above!

Thou art my reconcilèd Father, Thou!
Before whose awful throne those Seraphs bow,
Before whose glorious stupendous light,
The wingèd Cherubim must veil the sight.

Thou art my reconciling Saviour, Thou!
Who by that throne art interceding now,
Whom, though I see Thee not, I pant to love,
To view Thy glory, majesty above!

Thou art my Comforter! Great Spirit, Thou!
'Tis Thine with truth and wisdom to endow
The soul of man, and then to shed abroad
The peace, the knowledge, and the love of God.

My Father, Saviour, Comforter, my God!
Make Thou mine heart Thine honour'd blest abode,
Prepare me here on earth for heaven above,
An endless life of everlasting love!

Thou art my Praise.

"He is thy praise, He is thy God."
                              Deuteronomy x. 21.

Exodus xv. 26.   Jeremiah xvii. 14.   Psalm ciii. 3.   Psalm cxlvii. 3, 4.

THOU art my Praise!   Thou art my God!
   By terrible and mighty things,
Thine all-controlling righteous rod
   Deliverance and healing brings.

The God who pardons, pities, heals,
   Binds up the broken, bleeding heart;
Each wondrous page the truth reveals,
   The sacred scroll in every part.

Who tellest, as they roll along
   The glowing firmamental frame
Hymning their everlasting song,
   The stars, their number and their name.

Thou art my God!   Thou art my Praise!
   In every age and clime the same
This song of gratitude I raise,
   Jesus, to Thine exalted Name!

Image of God invisible![a]
   Thy Father's glory in Thy face!
Shield of pure gold invincible!
   Pavilion, Bower, and Rock of Grace!

THOU ART MY PRAISE.

The fulness of the Godhead dwelt [b]
   In Thee, before the worlds began;
Bright Seraphs at the threshold knelt,
   When, Virgin-born, revealed as Man.

God manifested in the flesh,
   Emmanuel! we hail the Name!
Recount th' angelic tale afresh,
   Again the joyous song proclaim.

Christ Jesus! Saviour, Lord and King!
   The glorious anthem rang and ran:
"Glory to God on high!" they sing,
   "Peace and good will on earth to man."

O! who the mystery may trace,
   What intellect, or tongue, or pen?
The mystery of Gospel grace
   B'yond mortal or immortal ken.

O! who may e'er exhaust the theme,
   May sound the dazzling depths unknown—
The intellect and heart supreme
   Of Everlasting Love alone?

Blest Father, Holy Spirit, Word!
   None may with Thee divide the fame;
God over all, Jehovah, Lord,—
   Thine incommunicable Name!

[a] Col. i. 15: Heb. i. 3.   [b] Col. i. 19; ii. 9.

Adoration.

"Thee would I adore, Almighty Father! To Thee I offer up my heart, and my soul's aspirations are breathed forth unto Thee! I am as nothing before Thee, O! everlasting Majesty!"—FENELON'S MEDITATIONS.

THEE would I love, Almighty Father, Thee!
   Who reignest on eternity's vast throne!
Thine own adopted one I seek to be:
   Thee would I love, "my Lord, my God," alone.

Oh! whom have I but Thee in heaven above?
   Whom upon earth but Thee should I desire?
What tongue may tell Thine all-surpassing love?
   What heart may know the bliss Thou can'st inspire?

Give me, great God, a humble holy heart,
   A mind endowed with wisdom from above,
Sin-conquering grace and courage true impart,
   And steadfast faith to live and work by love.

With Thy rich goodness my poor spirit fill,
   My conscience purge and cleanse from every stain,
Calm my wild thoughts, subdue my rebel will,
   The direful malice of my foes restrain.

ADORATION.

Thou art my Rock! Thou art my hiding-place!
   My harbour-refuge and my lofty tower!
I flee to Thee to hide me, God of grace!
   From sin and Satan's soul-destroying power.

Exalted Jesus! from the depths I cry,
   From deepest depths of sin and shame and woe:
Bow down Thine ear, turn Thy soft gracious eye,
   Prostrate I kneel Thy blood-stained cross below.

Eternal Comforter! descend, and bring
   And breathe around the soul-reviving calm;
Peace-speaking Spirit! stay Thy shadowing wing,
   To every wound apply the healing balm.

So shall I love my God! th' Eternal Three!
   And stand before the glorious crystal-throne,
Thine own redeemed and ransomed one to be,
   And praise for ever Thee,—my God alone!

"The Sons of God."

PSALM LVII. 7, 8.

AKE harp and lute to melody and song!
    To Him who loved me, and in His own blood
Hath washed and cleansed me, that I might belong
    To that bright company—" The Sons of God."

Who ever stand before His glorious throne
    Clothed in rich raiment and with harps of gold,
Sing their glad songs of love to Him alone,
    Whose matchless love hath never yet been told.

To that most Gracious Father who hath given
    His own loved Son for sinful man to die,
To raise us, grovelling in the dust, to heaven,
    To share His glory everlastingly.

To that kind Spirit, by whose gentle aid
    Our sin-bound souls, deep plunged in darkest night,
Have been delivered, and shall yet be made
    " Meet for th' inheritance of saints in light."

PRAISE.

Awake, my lute and harp, my heart, oh sing!
   Lift up thy voice, my soul, in shouts of praise;
To swell the strain attun'd be every string,
   And every nerve unite the song to raise,—

Of glory, gratitude, and glowing love
   To sovereign grace through rich redeeming blood,
To Father, Son, and Holy Ghost above,
   The Holy, Holy, Holy Triune God!

Praise.

"I will praise the name of God with a song, and will magnify Him with thanksgiving."

                                Psalm lxix. 30.

TO God be all glory, to God be all praise!
   A song of thanksgiving to God I would raise,
Who His blessings and mercies of grace and of love
   In bright golden showers[a] hath poured from above.

PRAISE.

If at times the blue firmament seemed overhung
With dark clouds, which but few bright spots were seen
    among,
How quickly they vanished, dispersed, and gave way
'Neath the cloud-melting beam and the gloom-piercing ray.

If at times the wild tempest with havoc laid waste
The fair face of nature, how soon 'twas replac'd;
Far, far brighter prospects and scenes were restor'd
By the breath, and the glance, and the smile of the Lord.

If at times the dread pestilence hovered around,
By its withering blast bearing all to the ground,
The life-giving Spirit of God [b] speeding forth
Hath revived and renewed a more glorious birth.

And oh! if at times my faint soul hath been clouded,
By doubt, or despair, or despondency shrouded,
Soon, soon have a joy and a peace been restor'd
By the mercy, the grace, and the love of the Lord.

Then to God be all glory, to God be all praise!
My song of thanksgiving to Him I must raise,
Who His mercies, His blessings, His grace, and His love,
In bright golden showers [c] still pours from above.

    [a] Ez. xxxiv. 26.   [b] Ps. civ. 30.   [c] Ez. xxxiv. 26.

The Eagle-Flight.

"*They shall mount up with wings as eagles.*" [a]

Isaiah xl. 31.

OH! there are moments when, elate with joy,
    The soul would wing aloft her heav'nward flight;
Her faith-illumined vision would employ
O'er blissful regions in the realms of light;
While Hope, the fair one, with irradiant smiles,
For the blest moments all the heart beguiles.

As the young eaglets mounting up to heaven,
    Exulting in their strength with buoyant gladness,
So to the soul the wondrous impulse given,
    She blithely soars above the clouds of sadness;
To revel in that freer, purer air,
And quaff the joy and bliss that meet her there.

[a] "But within every human breast there are capabilities of heaven, *folded wings of thought*, inspiration, energy, which need only the liberating touch of the Spirit of God to call forth their hidden power, and bear the soul upward to the true region of its life."—*Sermon on the Christian Heritage, in an admirable volume by the Rev. John Caird.*

THE EAGLE-FLIGHT.

All weariness and faintness left below,
   New vigour, energy, and life abound;
Through every vein delicious raptures flow,
   Celestial music seems to float around;—
For all is peace, and buoyancy, and love,
In the cerulean atmosphere above.

So sang th' inspired Prophet-bard of old,
   When, to his soaring spirit's gaze entranced,
The High and Lofty One vouchsafed t' unfold
   Veiled mysteries. Across his soul there glanced
A ray of bliss,—the rich, reserved reward
Of those who should wait humbly on the Lord :—

Who, seated on eternity's dread throne,
   Invisible, Jehovah, Holy King!
In wondrous condescension looketh down
   On all who, prostrate, prayer and praises bring;
Who rideth on the chariots of the sky,
Heareth the poor and needy when they cry :—

Who casteth down the valiant, when they trust
   In hosts and armies panoplied in pride;
Causeth the beggar, grovelling in the dust,
   On the high places of the earth to ride;
He to the broken-hearted sends relief,
And stills the storms of sin, and sin-wrung grief.

. . . .

THE EAGLE-FLIGHT.

And when in *other* seasons sorrow's blast
    Hath swept across the tempest-driven soul,
And all her once calm sky is overcast
    With clouds of woes that seem to mock control,
The stricken breast, with bitter anguish riven,
Can scarce lift up one thought, one hope to heaven!—

Is there no darkness-penetrating Star,
    Whose radiant light comes piercing through the gloom?
Is there no wondrous "still small voice" from far,
    Which o'er the wild and crashing thunder-boom
Breaks on th' entrancèd ear with softest sound,
And bids the soul with hope revived to bound?

Yes! gentle calms mysteriously blending,
    Alternating with storms and tempests wild,
Lulled by the one, and to the other bending,
    Through all with hope of coming rest beguiled:—
As some fair bark, until all perils past,
Holds on her course, and reaches port at last.

So shall each heav'n-bound soul her course direct,—
    Hope at the helm, and keen-eyed Faith on watch
With steadfast gaze, each signal to inspect
    And the first speck of land in sight to catch,—
Then furling every sail, her anchor cast
In that blest port and harbour—Heaven, at last!

The Dove and the Ark.

POOR, weary bird! poor, fluttering, trembling
    dove!
  Beaten and driven by the rude harsh wind,
In vain thou soar'st around, beneath, above,
  A resting-place for thy tired feet to find:
Yet hast thou found one "little branch" of peace,
  Sweet, fresh, and fragrant, blossoming and green?
Ah! though wild gusts assail thee and increase,
  Thou'lt bear it safe and bravely,—well, I ween.
My soul! in that poor bird thyself behold
  Tost by the tempests o'er life's fitful sea;
Thy little branch "hold fast," right firmly hold,
  And quickly to thine ark for shelter flee.—
Flee to the blood-bedewed Gethsemane,
  There let thine aching feet find peaceful rest;
Then wing thy flight towards the blood-stained tree,—
  Deep in its sheltering branches build thy nest,
And in thy gracious Saviour's wounded [a] breast
  Thou'lt find a "hiding-place," for ever safe and blest!

[a] . . . . "close in that wounded side,
Where only broken hearts their sin and shame may hide."—
                        "*Christian Year.*"

Peace and Love.

" The love of Christ, which passeth knowledge."
Ephesians iii. 19.

" The peace of God, which passeth all understanding."
Philippians iv. 7.

THERE is a "peace which passeth understanding,"
    Which only those who seek the Lord may know;
For that great God who loveth large demanding,
    Can more than all we ask or think bestow.

In everything by prayer with glad thanksgiving
    The saints may all their meek requests make known;
Confiding in their God, the Ever-giving,
    May daily bend beneath His mercy-throne.

For, lo! their great "Redeemer, King, Creator,"—
    "The Prince of Peace," "the Lamb for sinners slain,"
Stands by that throne: their mighty Mediator,
    For them to intercede doth live and reign.

There is a "love which passeth comprehension,"
    Whose breadth, depth, length, and height the saints may know,—
"The love of Christ," whose wondrous condescension
    Moved Him to save lost man from endless woe.

Come, then, ye weary! come, ye sinners, hither!
  Here seek a Father's reconcilèd face;
Princes and beggars, rich and poor together,
  Come to the mercy-seat,—the throne of grace!

Come and be healed, accepted, and forgiven;
  Come and be washed in rich, sin-cleansing blood;
Come and be robed in righteousness of heaven;
  Come and be reconciled through Christ to God!

"Thy Word."

PSALM CXIX. 18, 89, 160, etc.

 KNOW that every word of Thine,
  O God, my God, is sure;
I find in truth's exhaustless mine
  Gold unalloyed and pure.

Thou hast established it of old,
  From everlasting age;
Prophets, Apostles, all have told
  In every sacred page.

Oft as the heavenly food I eat
  It doth rejoice my heart;

THY WORD.

Rich wine, sweet honey, milk, strong meat,
    Health to the soul impart.

Oh! how I love Thy wondrous law,
    Mine inward man's delight!
No mortal wisdom ever saw
    Such truth, so deep and bright.

The brightest lamp that ever shone
    To guide the wanderer's feet!
'Tis golden sun, and silvery moon,
    Fair day-star, soft and sweet.

Its entrance understanding gives:
    The simple mind hath light,
The dead soul wakes, revives, and lives,
    The blind receive their sight.

I search its truths: they testify
    Of HIM in whom are stor'd
The wealth of ocean, earth, and sky,
    The treasures[b] of the Lord.

In whom in hidden mines, lie deep
    Wisdom and knowledge rare,
More precious than earth's golden heap,
    Or worldling's silver share.

Oh! I had perished long ago,
    Ten thousand times and more,
'Mid dire afflictions, storms of woe,
    Dashed on destruction's shore.

THY WORD.

My fragile bark had soon been lost,
    O'er life's storm-troubled sea;
Sin-driven, baffled, tempest-tost,
    Wrecked irretrievably.

When Thou Thyself, ETERNAL WORD,
    "The Mighty One to save,"
Spakest,—the roaring tempest heard,
    Stilled was the surging wave.

Great was the soul-amazing calm,[c]
    O wonder-working Man!
"The peace of God," like heavenly balm,
    Quick through my spirit ran.

The love of Christ,[d] in depth and height
    And length and breadth unknown,
The Light[e]—the uncreated Light—
    Of God in Jesus shown.

These are the wonders of Thy Truth,
    The "good things" of Thy Word,
By which my soul renews her youth,[f]
    Like the young eaglet-bird.

And so again I upward soar,
    To Thy bright throne, my King!
And so I shall for evermore
    Praise, glorify, and sing.

[a] Jeremiah xv. 16.   [b] Colossians ii. 2, 3.
[c] Matthew viii. 23—27.   "καὶ ἐγένετο γαλήνη μεγάλη."
[d] Ephesians iii. 18, 19.   [e] 2 Corinthians iv. 6.   [f] Isaiah xl. 31.

Where art Thou?

"And the Lord called unto Adam, and said unto him, Where art thou?"

Genesis iii. 8—15.

ARK! the piercing voice of God!
   "Where art thou, O man?"
Gently through the glade HE trod,
   Wildly Adam ran.

"When I heard Thy voice I shook,
   Fled aghast, dismay'd;
For Thy gaze I might not brook,
   Naked, shamed, afraid."

"Naked? Who hath told thee so?
   Why art thou afraid?
Say, how camest thou to know?
   Hast thou disobeyed?"

"Lo, the woman! It was she
   Gave, and bade me eat;
Help-meet whom Thou gavest me,
   She betrayed my feet."

"What is this that thou hast done,
   Woman weak and frail?
Why dost *thou* My presence shun,
   Scared, dishevelled, pale?"

"Lo, the Serpent! He beguiled,
    Tempted, and deceived;
Subtilly he whispered, smiled,—
    Foolish, I believed."

. . . . .

Hear again God's gracious voice,
    Hear, O man, and live![a]
Hear, and let thy soul rejoice,
    Hear, and praises give.

Lo! that fragile woman's Seed
    Hath the serpent foiled;
Here is wisdom deep indeed,—
    Christ hath Satan spoiled!

When the time's ripe fulness came,[b]
    God sent forth His Son;
Born of woman pure He came,
    And our ransom won.

Christ hath foiled the Serpent's art,
    And restored our race;
Sing we all, with all the heart,
    His redeeming grace.

[a] Isaiah lv. 3.   [b] Galatians iv. 4, 5.

Glorious Liberty.

1 CORINTHIANS XV. 10.

"What every man is in God's sight, that is he and no more."—*St. Francis of Assini, Founder of Franciscan Order.*

YOU know not what a man may be,
    You know not what he is,
Until the Truth hath made him free,[a]—
    It all amounts to this:

In intellect, affection, will,
    In heart, and mind, and choice,
The soul is but obeying still
    The subtil Serpent's voice.

But let the man be born again[b]
    Of God the Spirit's grace,
The former things are void and vain,
    The new the old efface.

'Tis when the love of Christ is known,
    And felt within the soul,
The love of sin is overthrown,
    The man is now "made whole."

GLORIOUS LIBERTY.

Now he is Christ's free man indeed,
   His servant, slave in love;
From fear, and death, and bondage freed,
   By freedom from above.

The dead in trespasses and sin
   In Christ now live and move;
His royal law engraved within,
   Brings liberty and love.

High love to God, kind love to man,
   With peace and pardon sealed:
The Gospel's grand eternal plan,
   In Christ's bright life revealed.

[a] John viii. 32, 34, 36.
[b] John iii. 3, 5, 6, 8; 2 Corinthians v. 17.

A Spiritual Song and Psalm of Life.

ROM. VII. 24.   1 COR. XV. 53—57.

TELL me not in flowing numbers
    That this fleeting life is all;
Sorely me, alas, encumbers
    Sin and death's funereal pall.

I would fain indeed disrobe me
    Of the grave-clothes of my guilt;
Great Chirurgeon! search and probe me,
    Cleanse and heal me, "if Thou wilt."

Bring me out of sin's dark prison,
    Charnel-house of death and shame,
Who in Thine own strength hast risen,
    "Resurrection," Thy blest name.

This dark life is death, and burneth
    Quicker than the taper's flame;
Dust to its own dust returneth,
    Lo! man's sin-achievèd fame.

All is vanity, vexation,
    From the cradle to the grave;
And the spirit's desperation
    Madly more and more will crave.

A SPIRITUAL SONG AND PSALM OF LIFE.

"Give me power, give me pleasure,
   And intoxicate me deep;
Give me earth-dug dross and treasure,
   Then for ever let me sleep."

O my brothers! come consenting,
   Hear the sweet evangel-voice;
God is waiting, haste, repenting,
   Angels o'er us shall rejoice.

Heavenward then their glad way winging,—
   Golden streets now daily trod,—
Joyously exulting, singing;
   "One more soul is won to God."

Heaven and hell are hourly filling
   With the wicked and the good,
While the Christ stands ever willing
   Sin to wash away with blood:

Blood that purgeth, cleanseth, healeth
   From the shame, the death, the sting,
And the Spirit quickly sealeth,
   Hovering on His gracious wing.

Rouse thee, rouse thee, sin-drugged sleeper!
   Christ shall give thee living light;
Madman! wilt thou plunge thee deeper
   In Gehenna's lurid night?

A SPIRITUAL SONG AND PSALM OF LIFE.

Fool! sleep on, the cup thou'st taken
   Soon must choke thy gasping breath;
Eheu! soon in hell thou'lt waken,
   Sleep the sleepless sleep of death!

Oh! my brother, I must wake thee
   From thy syren-poisoned rest,
Ere th' Archangel's trumpet shake thee
   Naked, speechless, unconfest![a]

Man immortal! rise sublimely,
   Be "a living soul" to-day;
All unseemly, all untimely
   Sloth and folly cast away.

Be Christ's true enlisted soldier,—
   Soldier of the Cross and Crown!
Bravely onward, and still bolder
   Hunt and hew the Tempter down.

Lay thee hold on life eternal,
   Strong, courageous in the Lord;
Slay thy lusts and foes infernal
   With the Spirit's two-edged sword.

Don the helmet of salvation
   In Jehovah's name and might;
On with earnest desperation,
   Bear thee bravely in the fight!

A SPIRITUAL SONG AND PSALM OF LIFE.

Take the breastplate tried that gleameth
    Bright with righteousness Divine;
Coat of mail, with truth that beameth,
    Gird thee hip and thigh and loin.

Bind on sandals of the Gospel
    Of good-will and peace to man,—
Angel-sung-and-hymned evangel:
    God's high-glory-giving plan!

Grasp the shield of faith, and dip it
    In the blood of God's own Lamb!
Heaven assault, and storm and win it,
    Bold in Christ, the great "I AM!"

Man of God! O man immortal!
    Be Christ's hero in the strife;
Enter through the living portal,
    Through the golden gate of life.

Comrades! men-at-arms of Jesus!
    From His throne's exalted height,
He beholds, descries, and sees us,
    How we bear us in the fight.

Knights of Calvary and Zion!
    Keen of glance the battle scan,
In the might of Judah's Lion,
    Lance in rest, lead on the van.

A SPIRITUAL SONG AND PSALM OF LIFE.

On right-hand and left assaulting,
    Fierce assailing front and rear,
Ever watchful for our halting,
    Satan daringly draws near.

"Principalities and powers,"
    "Wicked spirits" dark and bold,
Fiery darts in hurtling showers,—
    Perils, fightings, fears untold!

Nerve ye for the grand encounter,—
    Closing combat in the strife!
Strong in faith, each brave surmounter
    Shall receive "The Crown of Life!"

When our Captain, King, and Saviour,
    Who Himself hath fought and won,
Each shall greet with royal favour,—
    "Brave and faithful one, well done!"

---

[a] To guard against any misunderstanding of this expression in these days of "garbling," I would notify that the *confession* I point to, is that taught by the beloved Apostle, in 1 John i. 9, in connection with the *advocacy* of the "Great High Priest, that is passed into the heavens, Jesus the Son of God," as set forth in Hebrews ii. 17, 18, and iv. 14—16. And the throne of Grace is the true *confessional* for every sin-disquieted conscience.—*I know no other.*

No Cross! No Crown!!

O Cross, no Crown,—ah! must it be?
Is it our Father's wise decree?
The road that leads to heaven and God
Must it in sorrow oft be trod?

May no sequestered path be found,
No hallowed spot, no holy ground,
Where the tired pilgrim's foot may rest,
Nor by the lurking thorn be prest?

Doth the rude brier on every hand
The traveller's anxious care demand?
And as our steps we homeward bend,
Must we o'er rugged steeps ascend?

"Excelsior!"[a] then, our motto cry!
Our gaze still fixed on Calvary,[b]—
The plaited thorn, the blood-stained tree:
Cross, Crown, and Glory, all we see.

[a] Longfellow's exquisite little poem.

[b] ".......The Cross, on Calvary
    Uplifted high,
Beams on the Martyr-host: a beacon light
    In open fight."
        Christian Year, Wednesday after Easter.

"He restoreth my soul."

MICAH VII. 7—9.

AGAIN I rise
    And lift mine eyes,
    Rejoice not, O my foe:
    Though deep laid low,
My God and Saviour hath my soul restor'd,
Who from of old is Everlasting Lord!

    He fainteth not,[a]
    Nor hath forgot
    His own great Name and might,
    Nor "cast out" quite
The wretched, bruised and broken, crush'd and torn,
Nor left me yet forsaken, lost, forlorn.

    Though I must bear
    Keen anguish rare,
    His indignation dire—
    "Consuming Fire"—
My bones shall yet rejoice and shout and sing,[b]
He doth Himself His own deliverance bring.

HE RESTORETH MY SOUL.

   The Great God Man
   Himself hath ran,
   And lowly stooped to raise ;
   O deepest praise
Be to His own exalted wondrous fame,— .
"The Man Christ Jesus," He of noblest Name ![c]

   Of Him I'll boast,[d]
   And laugh almost
   With soul-exulting gladness ;
   My bitter sadness,
Now turned to joy, my mourning into dancing
By smiles of love my astonied soul entrancing.

   How strange to weep !
   Yet joy so deep
   O'erflows in sweetest tears ;—
   Dread thunder fears,
Wild wrath in the red flashing lightning gleaming
Are—where ? Cerulean peace with smiles is beaming !

   To weep how strange !
   Such rich exchange,
   Of terror, trouble, storm,
   Who could transform ?
But He who walked o'er Galilee's wild wave,[e]
The radiant-robed, the Mighty One to save !

HE RESTORETH MY SOUL.

His Sovereign will,
Grand "Peace be still,"
Wild storms rebuke and hush;
Soft wavelets gush
And kiss and play around those shining feet,
That brow encrowning, zephyred tempests meet!

To Him belong
My heart and song,
My life, my love, my praise;
And I must raise
My spirit's voice, and sing and tell His fame,—
Jesus! The First, the Last, His God-born Name,
"Yesterday, to-day, for ever, still the same."

^a Isaiah xl. 28—31.   ^b Psalm xxxv. 10.

^c 1 Timothy ii. 5.   Philippians ii. 9.   Ephesians i. 21.

^d Psalm xxx. 11, 12; xxxiv. 2.

^e John vi. 19, 20, and compare with Matthew viii. 23—27. Mark iv. 37—41. Luke viii. 22—25.

^f Hebrews xiii. 8. Isaiah ix. 6; xli. 4; xliv. 6; xlviii. 12. Revelation i. 8, 11; xxi. 6; xxii. 13.

Submission.

PSALM XLVI. 10.

" Be still, and know that I am God."

"BE still, and know that I am God,
    I will exalted be,"
Be humbled 'neath my chast'ning rod,
    My Great Salvation see.

'Tis not thine hand, nor thine own arm
    Can gain for thee renown;
I only can thy foes disarm
    And beat their malice down.

My holy arm, My strong right hand,
    My favour, and My grace,—
Deliverances I command
    From shame and dark disgrace.

O Lord of Hosts! Great Jacob's God!
    My King,—do Thou Thy will,—
I'd meekly bow and kiss Thy rod,
    Submissively "be still."

"Be Vigilant."

1 CORINTHIANS X. 12.

"Wherefore let him that thinketh he standeth take heed lest he fall."

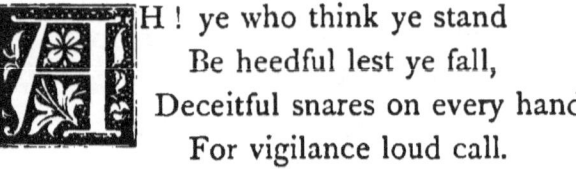H ! ye who think ye stand
    Be heedful lest ye fall,
Deceitful snares on every hand
    For vigilance loud call.

" Be not high-minded, fear,"
    The sacred precept saith,
Foes are around, storms may be near :
    Hold fast then by the faith.

The faith of God's brave saints,
    The justifying grace ;
Beware of counterfeiting feints,
    Masks of the One True Face.

To Jesus steadfast look,
    Cast every weight aside ;
Be every sin renounced, forsook,
    So faithfully abide.

Christ gives His glorious strength ;
    His grace upholds and guides ;
The victory shall crown at length,
    His power o'er all presides.

A Sacred Poem.

NCARNATE Holiness! Immortal Love!
Who, from the realms of glory bright above,
Cam'st down among the sons of earth to dwell,—
Thy matchless praises I aspire to tell,
The glories of Thy blest exalted Name,
Thy grace's trophies, triumphs of Thy fame.

I'd sing the virtues of Thy wondrous blood,—
Man's soul-redeeming, healing, cleansing flood,
Gethsemane's appalling crimson sweat
When the world's crimes o'er Thy bruised body met,
And o'er Thy spirit rolled so dire a grief,
An angel flew to minister relief.

The cruel scourge that purchased our release,
The stripes, the chastisement of all our peace,
By which Thy sacred flesh was gashed and torn,—
The brutal blasphemy, the taunt, the scorn,
The mockery, the spitting, and the shame,
The thorny crown,—of these I sing the fame.

A SACRED POEM.

The condemnation, which themselves condemned
And all their race with ruin overwhelm'd,—
The Lamb-like "Son of God!" who calmly stood,—
"The Son of Man!" the gentle, pure, and good,—
The wretched rabble, with the savage cry
"Away with Him! away to crucify!"

The Roman Ruler's witness,—"Lo, I bring,
Faultless! Behold the Man! Behold your King!"
"Away!" They force Him up the dolorous road,
While the fierce soldiers onward drag and goad;
See! see Him totter 'neath His load, and fall!
The sight might e'en those hardened men appall!

Upward they bear Him to the skull-strewn hill:
Meekly He yields Him to their savage will.
They strip, then fix Him to the cruel tree,
With hate-envenomed, mad, blood-thirsty glee,
Drive home the nail,—then raise the cross on high
And crowd around to see Him lingering die.

With diabolic cruelty accurst
They tempt His fevered, parching, burning thirst:
The sacred drops meanwhile are flowing down
From foot, and hand, and piercing thorny crown,
While here and there, in mocking groups there stand
Of Priests and Scribes a scornful, scoffing band.

A SACRED POEM.

But hark! What anguish'd wail, what bitter cry
Bursts from His lips to pierce the darkened sky?
("Eloi! Eloi! Lama Sabacthani!")
The boldest start and tremble.—"Stay! let be:
Whether Elias come, be still and see!"
No heaven-sent succour comes, no angel flies:
The God-and-man-forsaken Victim dies!

One last convulsive sob,—the dying wail!
Swift rent in twain the temple's symbol veil,
Earth reeled and shook, and with a roar of thunder
The rocks were rent, the graves were torn asunder
When the great "Son of God" gave up the ghost,
And sin, and death, and hell their empire lost.

These are the wonders that employ my song,
But to no mortal harp such themes belong;
By heavenly harpers, with their harps of gold
The glories of redemption must be told,—
The Lamb's own song, and all His praises sung
The blood-bought saints and angel-choirs among.
Faint is the spark from those ethereal fires
Which glow before the throne, my muse inspires,
My lyre unstrung falls from my drooping hand:
How can I sing *their* songs in *this* strange land!

Incarnate Holiness! Immortal Love!
Who, from Thy throne of glory bright above,

A SACRED POEM.

Cam'st down among the sons of earth to dwell,—
Forgive! that I presume Thy praise to tell;
No more to sing Thy fame I dare aspire,—
The heavenly theme with earth's unhallow'd fire.
Thy matchless praises, Thine exalted Name,
A Seraph's harp scarce worthy to proclaim!
Silent I fall: no more presume to sing,—
But all my homage, all my worship bring
Before Thy throne of light, O great salvation's King!

"Yesterday, and To-day, and for Ever."

PSALM LXV. 2, AND PSALM LXXVII. 19.

THOU prayer-hearing, peace-answering God!
Thro' the deep waters Thy bright feet have trod,
Oceans and seas are Thy pathway alone,
Yet are Thy footsteps unseen, and unknown.

Mountains bow down 'neath Thy swift burning feet,
Whirlwinds and tempests as dust-clouds retreat:
Thunder—Thy voice, gleaming lightning—Thine eye,
Robed in the azure and gold of the sky!

Deep in sweet Mary's womb hiding Thy might,
Gilding with glory red Calvary's height,
Bursting asunder the bars of the grave,
Thro' the abyssmal deep, "Mighty to save!"

Gone up on high, where of old Thou hast reigned,
"Leading captivity captive" enchained;
ᵃ Gifts Thou hast with Thee for rebels and free,
"Gifts in the Man" who was nailed to the tree!

YESTERDAY, AND TO-DAY, AND FOR EVER.

Gifts of salvation, redemption, and life;
Sceptres and crowns with rich jewell'ry rife;
Bright immortality, honour, and truth;
Brave, everlasting, free, glorious youth!

Soon now returning victorious and grand!
All the assembled before Thee must stand,
Bared in their shame, or in glorious robes,
While Thy bright piercing eye ev'ry heart probes.

Omega, Alpha! the First and the Last!
King, Prince, and Priest [b] of the present and past!
Prophets of old, in "dark sayings" proclaim,
Saints and Apostles re-echo the fame.

Sing, then, ye sons of God, joyous and free,
Lift up your heads, for how soon may ye see
Jesus—the Son of God, once on earth slain,
Jesus—the Son of man, coming to reign!

Soon may the bright azure curtain be furled,
Soon the usurper and tyrant down hurled;
[b] The Spirit and Bride both sing sweetly the strain,—
Jesus comes quickly, comes quickly to reign!

[a] Psalm lxviii. 18.

[b] Psalm cx. 4.   Heb. v. 6; vii. 17, 21.   Rev. xxii. 17.

"Wonderful."

ISAIAH IX. 6. MARK IV. 37—41.

ORKER of wonders! majestic and meek!
Ruling the tempests, assuring the weak,—
Walking o'er waters, so calm and so brave,
Glorious Rebuker of wind and of wave!

Calmly asleep in the midst of the storm,
Wonderful manner of man to perform,—
Miracle-worker, whom all must obey,
Tempests and devils both own Thy grand sway.

Great was the calm! when Thy Sovereign will
Breathed the deep "Peace," and soft-whispered "Be still!"
Faithless ones, be not afraid: it is I
Who gently, benignly, and brightly draw nigh.

Great was the calm in each terror-struck soul!
Thou art as mighty, Lord, now to control
Fears and temptations, without and within,—
Tempests of trial, and storm-blasts of sin.

Still in Thy meekness and mercy the same;
Jesus, Thy noble and wonderful Name!
Omega, Alpha, the First and the Last,—
Lord of the present, the future, the past!

"Bought with a Price."

"What shall a man give in exchange for his soul?"
Matthew xvi. 26.

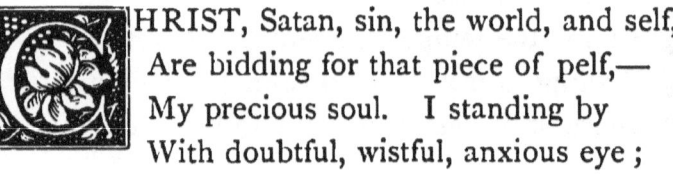

CHRIST, Satan, sin, the world, and self,
Are bidding for that piece of pelf,—
My precious soul. I standing by
With doubtful, wistful, anxious eye ;
For that small soul to me is worth
(Being immortal by its birth)
More than the world itself can hold
Of honour, treasure, pleasure, gold !—
Which of the bidders then shall I
Accept ? Stay,—did not Christ me buy
With His own precious blood's rich price ?
'Twould be a costly sacrifice,
I cannot, may not think of twice,—
To sell myself for *less*. Come in ^a
Dear Lord !—Avaunt ! world, satan, sin,—
I hate your clashing, cov'tous, clam'rous din !

^a Rev. iii. 2.   1 Cor. xi. 9.

"Issues of Life."

PROVERBS IV. 23.   ECCLESIASTICUS XIX. 1.

....*"He that contemneth small things, shall fall by little and little."*

CHECK the first beginnings,
    Quickly as they rise ;
Wash away thy sinnings
    From thy heart and eyes :
O keep diligently,
    Young man, guard thy heart ;
Round thee pestilently
    Hurtleth many a dart.

    Bind thee on, as frontlets,
        Christ's own sweet commands ;[a]
    Let them be as gauntlets
        To defend thy hands.
    Fierce destruction stalketh [b]
        In the broad noon-day ;
    The crafty fowler walketh
        To ensnare the prey.

ISSUES OF LIFE.

Turn thee from the stranger
   Who, with honeyed lip,
Lures thee to endanger,
   And would bid thee sip
Gilded bowls of pleasure,
   Poisoned unto death,
Which, with sudden seizure,
   Shall exhaust thy breath.

Fraud and shame and lying—
   Unseen shot and shell,
Thick around are flying—
   Artillery of hell;
Wild, unhallowed fires
   Flash from many an urn;
Foul, unchaste desires,
   Hidden, smouldering burn.

Seek the blest protection
   Of the Lord Most High!
Deadly foul infection
   Shall not then come nigh;
Safely and securely,
   'Neath th' Almighty shade,
Shall he lodge who, surely,
   Hath his refuge made:—

Built his habitation
   'Neath the shelt'ring wing
Of the Lord's salvation,—
   Rock and Living Spring:

ISSUES OF LIFE.

Plague and death dispelling
    Angels guard shall keep;
In his peaceful dwelling
    Calmly may he sleep.

Brother-saint! then, call thee
    Bravely on the Lord;
Harm shall not befall thee,—
    He shall help afford;
God shall thee ennoble,
    And thy foes destroy;
"In the day of trouble"
    He shall be thy Joy.

He shall thee deliver,
    And shall satisfy
With long life for ever;
    Thou shalt glorify
God, and His salvation,
    And with triumph sing,
With blest adoration,
    Christ, thy Saviour-King!

[a] 1 John v. 3.   [b] Psalm xci. *passim.*

A Spiritual Song.

1 JOHN I. 7.

AH! it is not my prayers that can save me,
    Nor my tears, supplications, nor cries;
But 'tis in that rich blood I must lave me,
    Which the love of my Saviour supplies.

It is this that alone can restore me
    To purity, calmness, and peace;
And as the warm stream [a] floweth o'er me,
    Sin's delirium and fever shall cease.

Here, here, would I daily be kneeling,
    At the foot of Redemption's blest tree;
And wait for the kind Spirit's sealing
    Salvation and pardon to me.

On Calvary, loftiest of mountains!
    In Gethsemane's sin-hiding shade!
At the purest and freest of fountains!
    By the tomb where Emmanuel was laid!

Hither haste thee, my soul, and alight thee;
    Here only thy feet shall find rest,
While joy and grief mingled delight thee,
    And a hope of the bliss of the blest.

[a] "And fresh, as when it first was shed,
    Springs forth the Saviour's blood."
—*Christian Year:* 18th Sunday after Trinity: 5th verse.

"God Manifest in the Flesh."

JOB IX. 10, 12; XIII. 15, 16; XXXVI. 22.

"*Which doeth great things past finding out; yea, and wonders without number.*"

"*Who will say unto Him, what doest Thou?*"

"*Though He slay me, yet will I trust in Him.*" "*He also shall be my salvation.*"

"*Who teacheth like Him?*"

"*Good and upright is the Lord: therefore will He teach sinners in the way.*"

. . . ."*Him shall He teach in the way He shall choose.*"

Psalm xxv. 8, 12.

"*Then will I teach transgressors Thy ways; and sinners shall be converted unto Thee.*"

Psalm li. 13.

[Once, after a very interesting conversation with a gracious lady, she turned to me and said (quoting, I think, a line from Tennyson's "*Princess*"),—"What woman taught you this?" Her remark awoke a train of thought, which resulted in the following lines.]

AH! 'twas no tender woman's heart that taught
    The deep and wondrous lessons I have learned;
No merely mortal hand the work hath wrought
    Whereby the Spirit's secret was discerned.

GOD MANIFEST IN THE FLESH.

" Himself hath done it : " His own " still small voice : "
   His " Peace ! be still," that calmed the threatening storm,
Hath bid the afflicted, tempest-tost rejoice,
   As through the darkness gleamed His radiant form !

Calm and majestic ! o'er the surging wave
   He held His own sublime triumphant way ;—
" 'Tis I : be not afraid," e'en I can save :
   The wondrous Man whom winds and waves obey ! [a]

Yes ! 'twas the Man of sorrows and of grief,
   Whose glorious heart with more than woman's love
O'erflows, who breathed the deep, rich, sweet relief,
   And sent the timely succour from above !

The great God-Man, both Human and Divine !
   Divine and Human, now for ever blent :
Almightiness and Gentleness combine
   In Him, who by the Father's love was sent.

The only wise, the true, eternal King [b]
   Veiled all His glory in the form of man,
Vouchsafed Himself the gracious news to bring,—
   Salvation's matchless mystery and plan !

God, in the flesh made manifest, revealed [c]
   The everlasting Truth and Life and Light :
The Hidden Wisdom, for long years concealed,
   In Christ broke forth, with chastened splendour bright !

GOD MANIFEST IN THE FLESH.

The Father's glory, full of truth and grace,[d]
    The light in whom th' Invisible is seen,
Shone clear in Jesus Christ's meek, lowly face
    And gentle spirit, in man's form and mien.

Who tells the stars their numbers and their name,[e]
    He to the broken-hearted breathes relief;
Whose voice is thunder, and whose eye is flame,
    Binds up the wounded spirit, soothes its grief.

Wonderful, Counsellor, the mighty God,
    The everlasting Father, Prince of Peace:[f]
The path of human sorrow Thou hast trod;
    And Thou alone can'st bid soul-tempests cease.

To-day, for ever, yesterday the same,[g]
    The Holy Spirit's revelation saith,—
JESUS OF NAZARETH, Thy glorious name:
    Author, Beginner, Finisher of faith.[g]

That NAME I'd sing with loud exulting voice!
    Thou once despised, rejected Nazarene,
In Thee my soul shall glory, boast, rejoice;
    Thy great salvation now mine eyes have seen!

[a] Matthew viii. 27.   [b] 1 Timothy i. 17.   [c] 1 Timothy iii. 16.
[d] John i. 14.   [e] Psalm cxlvii. 3, 4.   [f] Isaiah ix. 6.
[g] Hebrews xii. 2; xiii. 8.

A Dialogue.

"AH! wherefore dost thou doubt,
   O thou of little faith?
I never will cast out:"
   'Tis thus the gracious Saviour saith.

"O Lord, I do believe,
   Help Thou mine unbelief;
O haste Thee to relieve,"—
   Sighs forth my soul in sin-wrung grief!

And still,—"Why weepest thou?
   What is it thou wouldst seek?
Tell me, what thinkest thou?"
   "I'd list to what my Lord would speak."

"Say, sinner, 'Lovest thou Me?'"
   "'My Lord, my God,' I call,
Gently reprovest Thou me;
   'I love Thee, Lord,—Thou knowest all.'"

See Matthew xiv. 31.   John vi. 37; xx. 13, 15, 27, 28; xxi. 17.

A Hymn.

JAMES I. 17.

"Every good and every perfect gift is from above."

FATHER of love and light!
God of all grace and might!
To Thee my soul I lift
For every perfect gift.

Give me Thy Spirit's grace,
My sin and shame t' efface,
My soul to cleanse and heal,
And Christ's sweet love reveal.

Give strength to bear my cross,
To count all else but loss;
Give me the sprinkled blood
To make my peace with God.

Give me the fire-proved gold [d]
Of worth and price untold,
Sweet ointment for my sight,
And raiment clean and white.

A HYMN.

Give me the crown at last,
At Thy blest feet to cast;
The golden harp, to sing
The praises of my King!

Give me the robe of light
With Thine own glory bright;
Give me Thine own new name
To share Thy throne and fame!

[a] Revelation iii. 18.   [b] Revelation ii. 17.

"Sing, O ye Heavens."

SING, O ye heavens! shout for joy, O earth!
    The blood of Jesus cleanseth man from sin!
O precious stream, of rare and priceless worth,
    To fill the soul with strange delights within.

Sing, O ye sinners! shout, ye sons of men!
    'Twas God's own Lamb! 'twas God's own wondrous
        blood,[a]
Whose virtue passeth an Archangel's ken,—
    His Church-redeeming, sanctifying flood!

Sing, ye blood-purchased, ransomed, and redeemed!
    Glad songs of joy and everlasting praise;
For you th' evangel-day hath dawned, and beamed
    Salvation's golden age of life and grace.

Onward to Salem, Zion's holy hill!
    To view the glory of th' enthronèd King!
Through th' emerald fields by many a crystal rill,
    Onward ye ransomed! shout for joy, and sing!

[a] John i. 29, 36. Act xx. 28. 1 Timothy iii. 16.

Tears.

H, there is something touching in a tear!
    To feel it slowly trickle down the cheek
O'er some departed joy or loved one's bier,
    Leaving behind its sorrow-soothing streak.

To mark the eye—now beaming bright and clear,
    Reflecting as it were e'en heaven's own light—
Dimmed by the gushing, overflowing tear:
    Ah! is it not a soul-subduing sight?

But tears are sacred, too: for "Jesus wept!"
    The streams of sadness o'er His face would roll;
And sorrow's scorching blast hath often swept
    Over His sinless, sympathizing soul.

And He it was who said,—"Who mourn and weep
    Are blest." 'Tis written too, and therefore sure,—
Who sow in tears shall a rich harvest reap
    Of joy unsullied, endless, deep, and pure.

But there's a tale I love to dwell upon,
    A tale of tears, and true,—I mean when she,
That sinful, sorrowful, repentant one,
    Knelt weeping at His feet most bitterly;

TEARS.

While with her tears she bathed those sacred feet,
    And wiped them with her long luxuriant hair;
And they—self-righteous ones—who sat at meat,
    Wondered that He her touch could even bear.

But Jesus pardoned! And as there she knelt,
    Trembling, and yet so bold, He softly spake
Such words as caused her very soul to melt:
    Fresh flowed her tears, as tho' her heart must break.

Tears are a fountain which hath many springs;—
    The calm warm breath of love, the blast of woe,
The inmost spirit's deep imaginings
    Oft cause the secret soothing waters flow.

What though the night be long and dark and drear,
    The Star must rise—bright harbinger of morn,—
Heaven's endless smile absorb earth's every tear,
    Grief die—and everlasting joy be born!

John xi. 35. Matt. v. 4. Psalm cxxvi. 5, 6. Luke vii. 36—50. Psalm xxx. 5. Revelation vii. 17. Isaiah xxv. 8. Revelation xxi. 4.

"Wrath of the Lamb." "The Terror of the Lord."

REVELATION VI. 16.   2 CORINTHIANS v. 11.

RATH of the Lamb! the terror of the Lord!
O brother, tremble at the awful word;
For who may stand in His soul-piercing sight,
When Judah's Lion riseth in His might?[a]

Shall not the nations tremble, reel, and quake,
Shall not the thrones and kingdoms totter, shake,—
When, in His majesty, their own true King[b]
Ariseth, His own righteousness to bring?

How shall the mighty, wealthy, wise, and great,
Who trusted in their own vain strength and state,
Call on the rocks and mountains them to hide,
Their vaunted bravery, their pomp and pride?

The humble, lowly, patient poor shall then
Be owned and honoured truest, noblest men;
The meek inherit new-made heavens and earth;
The golden age of righteousness have birth.

Thy King, O Zion! thine, Jerusalem!
The virgin-born, the Babe of Bethlehem!
The meek-and-lowly-hearted Prince and King!
"JESUS OF NAZARETH,"—the Name I sing,—

WRATH OF THE LAMB.

Shall in majestic glory, royal right,
Thronèd on clouds of world-illuming light
(Angelic legions swell His glittering train),
Triumphantly return, supreme to reign!

The servants, saints, and soldiers of the Lord
Shall then receive their blood-bought, bright reward;
As kings and priests to God, with glorious mirth [c]
Sing the Lamb's song, and reign with Him on earth.

False priests, false prophets then unmask'd shall stand,
A lie-believing,-loving, scornful band;
While from His presence, in most dread dismay,
Scoffers and unbelievers melt away!

That Prophet who *has* come, the great High Priest,[d]
By all be known—the greatest and the least!
One King, one Lord, one name ador'd, alone [e]
Exalted over all Jehovah's throne!

O break, O break, blest morn! bright holy day!
Ye waning shadows, flee, O flee away!
The Spirit and the Bride still softly sing,—
Bright Morning Star arise: Lord Jesus, come, O King! [f]

[a] Revelation v. 5, 6. [b] Jeremiah x. 7. Revelation xv. 3, 4.
[c] Revelation v. 10. [d] Hebrews iii. 1; viii. 1, 11.
[e] Zechariah xiv. 9. Isaiah ii. 11, 17. [f] Revelation xxii. 16, 17, 20.

"Blood of the Lamb."

REVELATION XII. 11.

LOOD of the Lamb! Divine, celestial blood!^a
Great ransom price, vast world-redeeming flood,
In rich profusion poured, sublimely shed
When God's own Victim on God's altar bled!

O wondrous blood-and-water mingled stream
(Blent, yet distinct, both purple, crystal gleam)!^b
To cleanse and purify, make sweet and fresh
The sin-soiled spirit and polluted flesh.

Blest Fountain opened for uncleanness, sin,
Whose penetrative force can reach within,
And, softly trickling, sprinkle all the soul,
The conscience purify, revive, control.

By this the saintly heroes overcame
Dragon and devil, flood, and fiery flame;
Loved not their lives; with last triumphant breath
Shouted of victory won, and sealed by death.

BLOOD OF THE LAMB.

By this heroic saints still overcome,
Swelling its trophies to that countless sum,—
From every nation, tongue, and clime and tribe,^c
Salvation to the Lamb's rich blood ascribe.

By this Divine and human priceless blood,
Man-ransoming and world-redeeming flood,
The "kings and priests to God" shall ever sing
The Lamb's own song,—the saints' and angels' King!

^a Acts xx. 28.   ^b John xix. 34.
^c Revelation vii. 9, 14 ; xv. 3.

The Hiding Place.

PSALM XLVI..10.　JOHN XIV. 1.

"Be still, and know that I am God."
" Ye believe in God, believe also in Me."

BE still, my soul! Trust in thy God;
   He shed His blood
  In sad Gethsemane
  And mournful Calvary;—
   O, the relief
   Of deep belief!
T' assuage and calm soul-shaking grief.

When heavy clouds begin to lower,
   And tempest's power
  To raise wild waves around,
  Whose raging, surging sound
   Strikes fear within;—
   When roars the din
Of inward soul-accusing sin;—

Then flee, my soul! Then haste away
   Without delay
  To thy safe hiding-place,[a]

THE HIDING PLACE.

Thy rock, and tower of grace,—
　　The riven side
　　Of Him who died,
But now is risen, and glorified!

He ever lives, and reigns on high!
　　　How can'st thou die?
　Though floods and waters drench,
　They may not, cannot quench [b]
　　　The fire of love
　　　Which glows above,
Whose warmth cold hearts and dead may prove.

Hither, poor dove! poor weary soul!
　　　Thy fears control;
　Here seek thy hiding-place,
　Thy rock and tower of grace;
　　　Here stay thee! Rest,
　　　And build thy nest
In Love's warm bosom,—Jesus' gentle breast! [c]

[a] Psalm xviii. 2; xxxii. 7.
[b] Song of Songs viii. 7. Romans viii. 35—39.
[c] John xiii. 23.

Heart Communings.

PSALM IV. 4.

"Commune with your own heart upon your bed, and be still."

IN the stillness of my chamber, and the silence of my soul,
There is a gentle voice that doth my wildest fears control,—
'Tis like the breath of summer, from many flowers bearing balm,
Or as the lull of stormy wind, succeeded by a calm.

It is the Gracious Spirit who, descending from above,
And bearing, like the dove of old, a little branch of love;
Still speaketh peace, and kindleth hope, and sheddeth all abroad,
Within my dull and frozen heart, the glowing love of God.

E'en as a voice of melody soft floating o'er the sea,
When winds and waves are hushed to rest, and sleep so peacefully,
It stealeth o'er my calmèd soul in cadence sweet and low,
As gentle zephyrs from the south, rich-perfume-laden, blow.

HEART-COMMUNINGS.

Oh! 'tis the peace that Jesus breathes,—foretaste of promised rest
To weary ones, athirst and faint, heart-burdened and distrest;
Refreshing as the streams that erst flowed in the desert land
When Faith obedient raised the arm and waived the mighty wand.

What though the roaring tempest howl, the earthquake's crashing shock [a]
May rend the mighty mountains, and old earth's foundations rock;
Yet more,—with wild devouring rage, and devastation dire,
May pass the scorching breath of flame, and blast of withering fire!

These all have past! and that dread sound from Sinai's cloud-capt height,
And visions too tremendous e'en for the favoured leader's sight,[b]
Have passed away,—and now there breathes a gentle still small voice,
And soul-entrancing sounds and sights bid trembling ones rejoice.[c]

Lift up, my soul, thine ardent gaze; lift up thy glance on high,—
Soon shall yon azure canopy—light curtain of the sky—
Like to a mighty parchment roll be furled and borne away;
O'er the enraptured view shall burst heaven's bright transcendent day!

[a] 1 Kings xix. 11, 12. [b] Hebrews xii. 21.
[c] Matthew xxviii. 1—10. Luke xxiv. John xx.

"A Broken Heart, O God!"

LAMENTATIONS I. 22.

"For my sighs are many, and my heart is faint."

Y sighs are many, and my heart is faint;
Almighty Saviour! hear my woe-wrung plaint;—
O shed one pardoning glance, my guilt forgive,
And heal my broken heart, and bid me live.

Wast not Thou once, Thyself, with "grief acquaint"?
Thy sighs were many, and Thy spirit faint,—
O, Man of Sorrows! by that agony
That shook Thy soul in sad Gethsemane;—

By every tear in that loved spot that fell;
By that deep woe no tongue may ever tell;
By sweat of blood!—thine earnest prayers and cries,—
Heal Thou my heart, my God, and hear my sighs.

Then bid that heart revive, in Thee rejoice;
Attune to deepest praise my spirit's voice;
Awake my soul with holy love to sing
To Thee, her hope and refuge, God and King!

Balm of Gilead.

PSALM XCIV. 19.

"*In the multitude of my thoughts within me Thy comforts delight my soul.*"

FT, in the multitude of my wild thoughts within me,
   Do Thy sweet comforts solace and delight my soul;
Oft doth Thy soothing voice, O Saviour, woo and win me
   To peace, and hope, and joy, and all dark fears control.

How oft, when desolate, "cast down, though not forsaken,"
   Hath Thy rich grace afforded succour and relief;
How oft, when by some sad or sudden fault o'ertaken,
   My heart hath been o'erwhelmed by woe, and shame, and grief:—

Hast Thou not raised me up, and whispered sweet forgiveness
   Through that pure stream gushing from out Thy wounded side?
That fountain, opened for all sin and foul uncleanness,
   That mingled "blood and water"—free salvation's tide!

BALM OF GILEAD.

Ah! yes, Thou kind, Thou great, compassionating Saviour!
   To Thee sweet mercies and forgivenesses belong,
When Thou vouchsafest me a smile of Thy bright favour
   My soul bursts forth in humble gratitude and song.

To Thee! for all Thy tender, wondrous loving-kindness!
   For the unsearchable rich treasures of Thy grace;
Abashed at my own heart's deceitfulness and blindness,
   I hide in deep confusion, and in shame my face.

Yet, Lord! to Thy dear Name I'd raise a song of gladness,—
   Of praise to Thy long-suffering, forbearing love;
Oft hast Thou soothed my wild heart's bitterness and sadness,—
   Soon to praise Thee, I hope, eternally above!

The Fruits of the Spirit.

1 CORINTHIANS XII. 31.   GALATIANS V. 22.

"*The fruits of the Spirit.*"

THE fruits of the Spirit! I covet them more
Than all the world's glittering, shadowy store,
Its riches, its pleasures, its pomp and parade—
The fruits of the Spirit :—for these I have pray'd ;
And He who delights to give more than we ask,
Shall fulfil His own goodness,—salvation's sweet task.

The fruits of the Spirit! Bright Faith, Hope and Love!
Celestial Sisters! God-born from above ;
Come smile on my soul, and my spirit embrace,
Then sweetly refresh me with rich wine of grace ;
While blithely I sing at the banquet divine,[a]
My Saviour! My King! My Beloved One is mine!

[a] Canticles ii. 4, 16.

A Lamb as it had been Slain.

REVELATIONS V. 6. ACTS II. 23; III. 15; V. 30; VII. 52.

"A Lamb as it had been slain."

"The Lamb slain from the foundation of the world."

SLAIN Lamb! I slew Thee;—yes, this cruel hand
    Is dyed with Thy dear blood;
Now self-condemned before Thy cross I stand,
    My bruised and wounded God!
My crimson sins and scarlet guilt have slain,
And crucified the Lamb of God again!

Yet, Precious Lamb! I fain would hope that Thou
    Wast sacrificed for me;
With bitter tears before Thy cross I bow—
    That " reconciling tree :"[a]
Where, clinging to Thy pierced and bleeding feet,
I may a just and pardoning Father meet.

A LAMB AS IT HAD BEEN SLAIN!

Sweet Lamb! O worthy, worthy to receive
        All saint and angel praise,
For "Thou wast slain for us," and our reprieve;
        We sinners, we shall raise
The song to Thee, who with Thy precious blood
Hast ransomed and redeemed our souls to God!

And we, as Kings and Priests, on earth shall reign,—
        Great Judah's Royal Lion!
With Thee, O Precious Lamb of God, once slain,—
        Th' eternal King of Zion![b]
Shall cast our golden crowns at Thy blest feet,
And with adoring songs Thy princely presence greet!

    [a] "If but one leaf she may from Thee
        Win of the reconciling tree."
    —*Christian Year*, 5th Sunday after Easter, 6th Stanza.

    [b] Revelations xiv. 1.

A Spiritual Ode.

ACTS V. 31.

PRINCE and Saviour! Priest and King!
Sacrificial praise I bring;
True allegiance I would pay,
Loyal, faithful, homage lay
At Thy feet, before Thy throne.
" Thou art worthy," Thou alone :
Honour, glory, strength are Thine;
Riches, blessings, fame Divine!

Lamb of God! blest sacrifice!
Thou hast paid the noble price:
By Thy life, Thy blood, Thy grace
Ransomed our sin-ruined race.
It is finished,—It is done,—
Righteousness and peace are one;[a]
Truth and mercy now have met:
God's own gift hath paid the debt.[b]

Holy God and Father! now
Boldly at Thy throne I bow:
Lo, I come to do Thy will,
Thine own work obey, fulfil;[c]

A SPIRITUAL ODE.

And on Him whom Thou hast sent—
God and man for ever blent—
I with heart and soul believe,
And Thy priceless gift receive.

Holy Spirit! I implore
Truth and teaching more and more,
Peace and wisdom from above,
Faith, and hope, and holy love.
Give the sound and sober mind,
By Thine own true grace refin'd;
All "the outward man" subdue,
All "the inward" one renew.

So, my soul, with joyful lays,
Spiritual songs, and praise,
In the Lord shall make her boast,—
Father, Son, and Holy Ghost,—
Everlasting God and Lord!
By angelic hosts ador'd,
And His glories ever sing—
Prince and Saviour! Priest and King!

[a] Psalm lxxxv. 10.   [b] Romans vi. 23.
[c] John vi. 29.   [d] 1 Timothy iii. 16.

The Great Brother!

PROVERBS XVII. 17; XVIII. 24.

"A friend loveth at all times, and a brother is born for adversity.....And there is a Friend that sticketh closer than a brother."

CHRISTIAN YEAR.   24th Sunday after Trinity, two last stanzas.

" But that Thou call'st us brethren, sweet repose
  Is in that word, the Lord who dwells on high
  Knows all, yet loves us better than He knows."

[This little piece was inscribed to the late Sir G—— B——, who died at the Great Western Hotel, in September, 1863. The writer was sitting by his bedside one day; when he suddenly, after a long pause and silence, exclaimed, " Then, in fact, Christ is our Brother ! "]

GREAT Brother, mine! I claim Thy gracious power,
  Now in adversity's dark, cloudy day,
When storms of fear, and dire temptations lower
  Around my sad, sin-desolated way.

My soul bowed down, my spirit sore opprest,
  Wild waves of trouble rolling, surging round;
While bitter memories still wring my breast,
  And present griefs combine to bruise and wound.

THE GREAT BROTHER.

Yet, gracious Brother! Sympathizing Friend![a]
   I fain would bring to Thy remembrance [b] kind,
How in past years Thou oftentimes would'st send
   And soothe the sorrows of the wounded mind.

And Thou art still the same,—I know Thou art!
   So I still cast me on Thy loving breast,—
The depths of Thy compassionating heart
   Shall yield me yet again balm, comfort, rest.

O Faithful Brother! hear my plea, still hear:
   Thou art my Friend! my Father too! my All!
Still comfort me, as mother [c] fond and dear
   Flies to relieve her infant's wailing call.

Let all forget me [d]—Brother! do not Thou!
   Thy gracious promise penetrates my heart;
From Thine own "everlasting love," [e] nor now,
   Nor ever, let aught sever us apart.

And oh! my Gracious Brother! I will give
   To Thee my heart's affection—all my love;
For Thee I'd die,[f]—and yet for Thee I'd live,
   For Thy dear Name,—all namèd names above![g]

[a] Hebrews iv. 15; xiii. 8. [b] Psalm xxv. 6, 7. [c] Isaiah lxvi. 13.
[d] Isaiah xlix. 15. [e] Jeremiah xxxi. 3; Romans viii. 35—39.
[f] John xiii. 37; Acts xxi. 13. [g] Ephesians i. 21; Philippians ii. 9.

"Who loved Me."

GALATIANS II. 20.

"The Son of God who loved me, and gave Himself for me."

AND didst Thou give Thyself for me,
And shall I aught withhold from Thee?
      My Saviour and my God!
Wast Thou on earth with grief acquaint,
Shall I then murmur, sigh, or faint
      Beneath Thy chastening rod?

Why doth my restless heart repine,—
Hast Thou not told me I am Thine,
      And that no power may sever
Me from Thine own all-conquering love;
That I shall rest with Thee above
      For ever, and for ever?

Subdue, dear Lord, this stormy heart,
Bid all its restlessness depart,
      And reign supreme, alone!
I would be still: do Thou fulfil
Thine own kind work, Thine own good will,
      And self and sin dethrone.

WHO LOVED ME.

Each hope, desire, and anxious thought,
Into captivity be brought
      To Thee, and thine obedience;[b]
Redeemed from bondage, I would bring
To Thee, my own true Lord and King,
      My willing glad allegiance.

Thee would I honour, serve, obey:
O guide me in the narrow way
      That leads to life above!
And as I rest, or run, or walk,
Be all my converse, all my talk
      Of Thee, and Thy deep love.

My mouth be filled with Thy sweet praise,
My gladdened soul break forth in lays
      Of joy and adoration;
Until, the victory gained at last,
At Thy bright feet my crown I cast,
      With shoutings of salvation!

[a] Song of Songs ii. 16. Romans viii. 37, 38, 39.
[b] 2 Corinthians x. 5.

A Song of Zion.

PSALM L. 14, 23; XLVII. 6, 7.

"*Offer unto God thanksgiving. Whoso offereth praise glorifieth Me.*"

"*Sing praises to God, sing praises; sing praises unto our King, sing praises. For God is the King of all the earth: sing ye praises with understanding.*"

HY waste ye, singers, heart and voice and song?
Why sing ye not of Him, to whom belong
All glory, beauty, majesty, and fame,
Alone exalted, excellent His Name![a]

Why waste ye genius, energy, and life
Upon the world's vain pomp, applause, and strife?
Oh, why not sanctify, devote the gift—
The voice, to Him who gave, in praises lift.

Young men and maidens, children, old and young,[b]
Let Hallelujahs loud, from every tongue,
In one triumphant peal of praise and song
Ascend to Him, to whom all gifts belong.

A SONG OF ZION.

Let the true science of the one " True God,^c
And Jesus Christ" be man's divining rod ;
And the high art of doing good to men
Adorn the pencil, and inspire the pen.

Brave music, song, and eloquence combine
To elevate the soul to things divine,
Enkindled with the flame of holy love
From the high altar by the throne above.

Science and learning, wisdom, riches, wealth,
Courage and vigour, strength, and youth, and health
Be hallowed to the service of the Lord,
Who gives the gifts, the blessings doth afford.

Then righteousness shall flourish in the earth,
Goodwill, and justice, peace, and holy mirth ;
In all the world wild, savage, warfare cease,
Beneath the sceptre of the " Prince of Peace."

The wolf and lamb may then together feed,^d
The little child the calf and lion lead,
Bright babes with harmless asps and adders play,
The kindly leopard seek the new-mown hay.

The knowledge of the Lord the whole earth fill,
All nations own, obey, and love His will ;
And He shall dwell with men, and be their God,^e
Who once for man the paths of sorrow trod.

A SONG OF ZION.

The Lord Himself be universal King ![f]
The King of righteouness, of whom I sing—
While all who bow beneath His gracious rod
Shall reign with Him, as " Kings and Priests to God."[g]

[a] Psalm cxlviii. 13, *margin*.   [b] Ibid 12.   [c] John xvii. 3.

[d] Isaiah xi. 6, 7, 8, 9 ; lxv. 25.

[e] Ezekiel xxxiv. 31.   Revelation xxi. 3.

[f] Zechariah xiv. 9.   [g] Revelation i. 6 ; v. 10 ; xx. 6.

"The Power of Christ."

2 CORINTHIANS XII. 9.

" My grace is sufficient for thee." " My strength is made perfect in weakness."

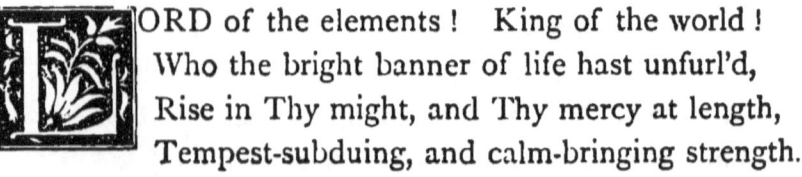

LORD of the elements ! King of the world !
Who the bright banner of life hast unfurl'd,
Rise in Thy might, and Thy mercy at length,
Tempest-subduing, and calm-bringing strength.

THE POWER OF CHRIST.

"Let God arise, and be scattered His foes,[a]—
All flee before Him who hate or oppose;"
While on the pinions of peace-breathing love
Soon may return His celestial Dove!

Set up Thy kingdom, Thy throne in my heart;
Bid the unclean one, the proud one depart:
Demon-rebuker! the wild one reclaim
At Thy blest feet to sit, gentle, and tame.

Oh! by that word "grace sufficeth for thee,"
From the vile thraldom of self set me free,
While the old devil, the world, and my sin
All be cast out, or subjected within.

Then to go forth, and exulting proclaim
Hither and thither, Thy marvellous fame!
While the sin-torn ones, tormented, and tost,
Hear of salvation, and life for the lost!

[a] Numbers x. 35, 36. Psalm lxviii. 1.

The City of God.

PSALM LXXXVII.

" Glorious things are spoken of thee, O city of God."

GLORIOUS things of thee are spoken,
   Zion, city of our God!
Never may thy peace be broken
   By th' oppressor's iron rod;
All thy bulwarks are salvation,
   And thy gates of pearl are praise,
And the blood-bought ransomed nation
   Sing thy sweet redemption lays.

In th' eternal holy mountains
   On "the Rock of Ages" built,
Whence there flow the living fountains
   And are hewn the streets of gilt;
Deep, immoveable foundations
   Rich with precious stones are laid,—
See the Patmos revelations,
   Read the glories there display'd.[a]

THE CITY OF GOD.

There too 't will be found, recorded
   In the registry on high,—
When, the royal gifts awarded
   'Neath the King's own gracious eye,
When His glory shines upon her
   With celestial beauty bright,—
This, and that man claim high honour,
   Citizens, by royal right.

Everlasting joy and gladness
   On their heads the saints shall bring,
Gloom and sorrow, sigh and sadness
   Into Hades' depths shall fling;
Then shall rise Jehovah's glory,—
   God, the Lamb, the living Light
Everlastingly shine o'er thee,
   In thy midst for ever bright!

[a] Revelations xxi. and xxii.

"Living Bread."

DEUTERONOMY VIII. 3.   MATTHEW IV. 4.

" Man doth not live by bread alone."

MAN doth not live by bread alone,—
    By every holy word of God
Men to their stature full have grown,
    And borne the pilgrim's staff and rod.

The very finest of the wheat,[a]
    The strengthening bread and wine of life,
Clear springs, pure milk, and rich strong meat,[b]
    With vigour, health, and spirit rife.

Than all the gold that e'er was wrought
    From ancient Ophir's famous mine,
More precious Thine unfathomed thought,[c]
    Thine utterances deep, divine.

Sweeter than droppings of the comb,[d]
    Its choicest honey to my mouth;
My treasure, food, where'er I roam,
    In bracing north, or glowing south.

LIVING BREAD.

My song upon my pilgrim way,
    Shall be the glories of Thy Word,—
With voice, and verse, in legend, lay,
    I'll tell the wonders I have heard.

That all may search the sacred rolls,
    Which testify, my Lord, of Thee,—
Those ancient, rich, inspired scrolls,
    Their hidden wisdom learn to see.

And the Great Spirit, good and true,
    Their eyes may ope, their hearts inflame,—
Reveal to their amazèd view
    The secret of Thy wondrous Name! [e]

[a] Isaiah lv. 1.   [b] Hebrews v. 14.   1 Peter ii. 2.
[c] Psalm xcii. 5 ; xl. 5.   Isaiah lv. 8.
[d] Psalm cxix. 72, 103 ; xix. 10.   [e] Judges xiii. 18.   Isaiah ix. 6.

"The Mount of God."

PSALM XI. 1.

"How say ye to my soul, flee as a bird to your mountain."

"HE Mount of God!" Mount Calvary I sing!
Where Jew and Gentile crucified their King,
The Lord of glory, Prince of life and peace,
Who brought redemption, ransom, and release.

There will I flee, and there my soul shall find
Security and rest, and peace of mind;
Nay, "Peace of God" that passeth human thought,
With sweet serenity and wisdom fraught.

O loftiest mountain! towering to the skies,
Crowned with a glory dazzling mortal eyes!
Ah, who may gaze upon *that* light and live,
Unless God's Spirit sight celestial give.

Then shall the glory of Jehovah burst
Forth in that face [a] so wondrous, yet so curst;
"Jesus of Nazareth" upon that tree,
The Jew, the Gentile—their Great King shall see.

Then every tongue confess that He is Lord—
He only shall exalted be, ador'd;
And as the waters cover, fill the sea,
Earth with God's glory covered o'er shall be!

[a] 2 Corinthians iv. 6.

A Spiritual Song.

EPHESIANS III. 8.

" The unsearchable riches of Christ."

HE unsearchable riches of Christ,
The unsearchable riches of Christ!
Ah, who may tell—rare Gospel-spell—
At what man's soul was pric'd.

The blood of His own dear Son,
The blood of His own dear Son!
The ransom was laid, and the price was paid,
And so man's soul was won.

A SPIRITUAL SONG.

O Love that is passing thought,
O Love that is passing thought!
Say, can it be so; yes, surely I know
That Christ my soul hath bought.

And now I am His alone,
And now I am His alone;
I'll live or die without sorrow or sigh,
For Christ is all my own.

His Spirit my soul hath wed,[a]
His Spirit my soul hath wed
To Christ my Lord; of His own accord
He loved me, and for me bled.

Now, glory to Christ my Lord,
Now, glory to Christ my Lord!
To Father, and Son, and Spirit in One
GOD! worthy to be ador'd!

[a] 1 Corinthians vi. 17.   2 Corinthians xi. 2.

A Contrast.

'VE seen the sun at dawn of day
    In bright effulgence rise,
Melting the clouds of night away,
    And gild the smiling skies.

So gently have I seen begin
    The morn of the softened heart,—
The night, the gloomy night of sin,
    With all its clouds depart.

I've seen the sun's meridian glow
    Set free the frost-bound earth,
Melting its winter garb of snow,
    And give the glad spring birth.

So have I seen the heart subdued,
    Its frozen soil unbound;
By the bright Sun of grace renewed,
    With hope and harvest crown'd.

A CONTRAST.

I've seen the sun at autumn's eve [a]
   Sink 'neath the western sky,
Behind its lingering splendour leave
   A chastened brilliancy.

So have I seen sink down to rest,
   So marked the good man die,
And caught a gleam of what the blest
   Enjoy of light on high.

   [a] " Ever the richest tenderest glow
      Sets round the autumn sun,
     But there sight fails : no heart may know
      The bliss when life is done."

              Christian Year, 22nd Sunday after Epiphany.

"Repentance to Salvation."

JEREMIAH IX. I.

"Oh, that my head were waters, and mine eyes a fountain of tears."

"OH, that my head were waters, and mine eyes a fount of tears!"
In penitential streams to flow when all my guilt appears:
When rising from the past's dark depths, like phantoms to dismay
My troubled soul, my sins pass by in terrible array!

Yet, could I weep an ocean, could my tears in rivers flow,
My burdened spirit's inmost thoughts break forth in groans of woe,—
Were day and night in anguish, and in bitter sorrow spent,
Would then my injured Lord forgive, my slighted God relent?

Could I an offering present in which He would delight,
A sacrifice acceptable, well-pleasing in His sight?
Could blood of bulls and goats atone for all my countless crimes,
Perverse transgressions multiplied ten thousand thousand times?

REPENTANCE TO SALVATION.

Ah, no! But yet methinks I've heard a tale of wondrous love,
Of One, a holy spotless Lamb, who came from heaven above;
Who, just, and pure, and innocent, poured out his own life's blood,—
A stream to wash away our guilt, a rich sin-cleansing flood!

Here then I'll flee, and prostrate fall beneath it flowing tide:
The blood and water gushing forth from Jesu's piercèd side
My scarlet sins shall whiter make than winter's purest snow,
And cause my once diseasèd soul with health and beauty glow!

O, melt my heart! Let mingling streams of humble joy and grief
From out thine inmost depths flow forth, and yield thee rich relief,
The blest relief of pardoned sin, thro' sin-atoning blood:
There mayest thou meekly claim the boon of " peace, thro' Christ, with God!"

Texts to prove the above. Micah vi. 6, 7. Hebrews x. 4. 1 Peter i. 19. John xix. 34. Isaiah i. 18. Romans v. 1, 9, 10. Colosians i. 20.

"He Careth for You."

PSALM CXLII. 3.

"When my spirit was overwhelmed within me, then Thou knewest my path."

CHRISTIAN YEAR.   Monday before Easter, 3rd stanza.

" O'er thee He watches in His boundless reign."

THERE is an Eye that watcheth o'er my path,
A gentle Voice that doth assuage my grief,
A refuge and a hiding place from wrath,
A balm to yield my wounded heart relief!

It is that gracious Eye all hearts beholding,
Of Him, exalted on the Mercy-throne—
Whose Holy Arm the universe upholding,
Yet raiseth each poor, burdened, prostrate one.

It is the still small soothing Voice of Jesus,
Which calms the roar of storm and wind and wave,
Rebukes the rage of tempests fierce, and frees us
From dread of overwhelming ocean-grave.

His wounded side a safe retreat still offers,
Where broken hearts may hide their sin and shame,[a]
To bruisèd spirits heavenly balm He proffers,
Thro' the rich healing of His blood and name![b]

HE CARETH FOR YOU.

Recall, my soul, those gracious words once spoken,—
" Thy sins are all forgiven, go in peace "—[c]
To her who knelt in heart and spirit broken,
Which gently bade her tears and terrors cease.

Like her, at Jesu's feet, with contrite spirit
With bitter flowing tears, bow down, my soul !
He heals the broken heart, and He can fill it
With peace and hope, and all its fears control.

Like her, who faintly crept to touch the border [d]
Of Jesu's garment—that blest, seamless robe—
Touch thou by faith ; so shall thy foul disorder
Be healed, and soothed its wildest, fiercest throb.

Tho' tempest tost, thou shalt not be forsaken,[e]
Thy God and Saviour ever is the same ;
Soon shalt thou rest in peace, and soon awaken
Sealed, saved, accepted in His glorious Name !

O, come, all weary wanderers to Jesus !
Come, and have all your sin and shame forgiven :
Who loved, and lived, and died for us, still sees us,
And He will give us rest, and peace, and heaven !

[a] " To that dear home, safe in Thy wounded side,
Where only broken hearts their sin and shame may hide."
Christian Year, Good Friday, last stanza.

[b] Song of Songs i. 3 :—" Thy name is as ointment poured forth."

[c] Luke vii. 37—50.   [d] Matthew ix. 20—22.   [e] Isaiah liv. 11.

"Glory in the Lord."

PSALM XXXIV. 2—4.

ES, in the Lord, my soul shall make her boast:
Come, all ye humble-minded ones, rejoice,
And strive with me to magnify Him most;
Yet loudest in the song (methinks) shall be my voice!

I sought the Lord, and graciously He hearkened,
Saved and delivered me from all my fear,
Dispelled the clouds that o'er my pathway darkened,
And bid the bright glad sun and sky again appear!

He,—Who in matchless, unexampled love,
Which passeth all the power of human thought,
Came down from His bright glory-throne above,
And paid the price by which immortal souls are bought.

The costly price! His own heart's precious blood!
Whose wondrous value angels may not know—
A world-embracing, and redeeming flood,
Whose life-imparting waters through all ages flow.

GLORY IN THE LORD.

All past, all present, and all future time
May not exhaust its healing virtues rare ;
From every tongue and nation, tribe and clime,
Poor sin-diseasèd souls may come and wash them *there!*

And through Eternity's unclouded day,
Basking beneath the warm celestial beam,
The happy saints shall ever swell the lay
Of praise, and find it still a never tiring theme : [a]—

On golden harps, shall raise the grand acclaim,
As through the burnished streets their path is trod,—
Of highest glory unto Jesu's Name,
Who washed and ransomed and redeemed their souls to
    God!

Psalm lxix. 30.   Revelations i. 5, 6 ; v. 8, 9 ; xxi. 21.

[a] . . . . The God who dwelt in man !
. . . .
How many centuries of joy concentrate in that theme !
Proverbial Philosophy, 2nd series, Immortality.

Leaning upon Her Beloved.

JOHN XIII. 23, 25; XIV.

LEANING on Jesu's bosom,
 Lying on Jesu's breast,
There is repose and peace for thee,—
 There, weary soul, thy rest!
Let not your heart be troubled;
 Oh! be not thou afraid:
Still trust in God, still trust in Me,
 For I thy peace have made.

For thee My heart was wounded,
 And pierced for thee My breast,—
My hands and feet, My bleeding side
 Thy refuge are, thy rest!
I leave thee this rich legacy
 The world could never give,
That thou may'st find thy peace in Me,—
 That thou in Me may'st live.

High in My Father's mansion
 I now prepare a place
For thee, and all My ransomed ones,—
 A beauteous home of grace!

LEANING UPON HER BELOVED.

And lo! I quickly come again:
   In *that* day thou shalt see
That thou, with all My ransomed ones,
   With Me shalt ever be.

Meanwhile I send the Spirit,
   And He shall take of Mine,
And testify to Thee of Me,
   And all My love divine;—
The Holy Ghost! the Comforter!
   Who shall My name reveal,
And to the great redemption day
   Thy soul in safety seal.

"Awake!"

PSALM LVII. 8.   EPHESIANS V. 14.   ISAIAH LI. 9; LII. 1, 2; XXVI. 19.

WAKE! my harp, awake!
The Spirit's breath shall shake
And strike thy silent chords again
To heav'n-ascending song and strain.

Wake! thou that sleepest, wake!
Ere black-winged death o'ertake,
Shake off the slumbers of the night,—
Arise, and Christ shall give thee light.

Awake! and put on strength,
O arm of God! at length,
Awake! as in the ancient days,
The generations of Thy praise.

Awake! O Zion, wake!
Thy dust-stained garments shake;
Put on thy beauty-robes again,—
Thy Lord and King returns to reign.

AWAKE!

Wake! slumbering virgins, wake!
Ere the last trumpet shake
Both heaven and earth.—Your lamps re-trim;
The Bridegroom comes! O, welcome Him!

Awake! awake! and sing,
Behold Redemption's King!
Ye sleeping saints awake, arise,
And swell the chorus of the skies!

"A little lower than the Angels."

HEBREWS II. 16—18.

"But the Son of God resolved from all eternity to die for sinners."—MᶜCHEYNE'S SERMONS.

H! glorious Son of God! I'd sing Thy praise:
Oh! gracious Son of Man! inspire my lays;
My spirit fill with holy hymn and song,
That I may tell the grace that doth to Thee belong.

'Twas not for Angels Thou didst stoop to die,
Thy matchless condescension passed them by;
Down to the depths of human shame and sin
Thou bow'dst Thy holy head, Salvation's crown to win.

Thou Gentle One! so gracious, meek, and lowly,
Riding on ass' colt, so calmly grand,
Art heav'n's Eternal King!—the High and Holy,
Before whose glory-throne the veilèd seraph stand.

May mortal tongue presume Thy praise to sing?
May "unclean lips" pronounce that wondrous Name?
May "dust and ashes," worthy homage bring?
Or earthly harp be tuned to hymn Redemption's fame?

A LITTLE LOWER THAN THE ANGELS.

The glories of the Cross and bleeding Lamb!
The victory o'er death and Satan won,
By God revealed in flesh,—the Great I AM!
The Sinless-born, and God's beloved Eternal Son!

Thou deignd'st to hide Thee in meek virgin's womb,
When Thou would'st ope the golden gate of life;
Thou wrestedst from the Spoiler in the tomb
His iron sceptre: glorious Victor in the strife!

"Strong Son of God!" Exalted Son of Man!
We *do* believe that Thou wilt come again
To crown Thy Great Salvation's royal plan,
And take Thy saints, with Thee in glory bright to reign!

"Is it True?"

The following lines were suggested by my hearing a young friend sing a plaintive song, the refrain of which appeared to take the form of the above words.

"IS it true?" May I believe the story—
    The wondrous tale of God the Father's love,
Graven in characters of blood and glory,
    And heralded to man from heav'n above.

"O, is it true?" that He, the High and Holy,
    Inhabiting Eternity's vast throne,
Revealed Himself on earth as " meek and lowly,"
    And God-in-Christ, Emmanuel was known.

"O, is it true?" that He will yet restore us
    To more than Eden's happiness of old ;
That in His boundless reign He watcheth o'er us,
    E'en as a tender shepherd doth his fold.

"O, is it true?" that God the Holy Spirit
    Within a mortal breast will deign to dwell,
By His rich grace prepare us to inherit
    The happy land, whose bliss no tongue may tell.

O yes! 'tis true! tho' heart may ne'er conceive it:
    Revealed to earth and known in heaven above,
In silent and adoring faith believe it,
    My Soul,—the truth of truths—that " God is Love."

"Hide Me."

PSALM CXXXIX. 7.

" Whither shall I go from Thy Spirit, or whither shall I flee from Thy presence."

IF through eternity's vast space,
   Unbounded, pathless, without trace,
   Where neither limit, confine, bound,
   Mark, sign, nor footstep may be found,
I roamèd far, to search if I
Might hide me from th' All-seeing eye;
Could I so hid, secreted be
As Omnipresence might not see?

If by some power borne on high,
Far, far above yon deep blue sky—
Say, on the wings of the mighty wind,—
Could I, 'mid other bright orbs, find
A spot so secretly unknown
Where I might hide me all alone;
Could I be hid so secretly
As that Omniscience should not see?

HIDE ME.

If by that power, resistless hurl'd
Down far beneath this atom world,
Deep in the fathomless depths of hell,—
Could I alone in secret dwell,
In night impenetrable hid,
Blackness and darkness, clouds amid,—
Say, could I then so hidden be
That Omnipresence might not see?

If, on the wings of early morn
O'er ocean's wide, wild bosom borne,
Where neither track nor trace is known,
Could I be left unseen, alone;
Or lifted high on her billowy crest,
Or buried deep in her mighty breast,—
Could I, e'en then, so hidden be
As that Omniscience should not see?

Is there a realm where broods black night
So dark that e'en all-piercing sight
Nor penetrates, nor aught can see,
Where I at last might hidden be
In endless solitude, unknown,
And everlastingly alone!
Where I at last might hidden be,
And Omnipresence never see?

AMBITION.

No! I may never be alone!
Nor hide me from th' Omniscient One;
Nor heaven, nor hell, nor day, nor night,
Nor earth, nor ocean, dark nor light
May screen me from th' All-seeing eye
Of Him,—the Holy and the High;
Then let me hide myself in Thee,
My God, for all Eternity!

Ambition.

EARTHLY.   HEAVENLY.

AMBITION still is lurking
    Within my stirring breast,
And subtilly is working
    The poison of unrest;
Its whisper,—" Up: be doing,
    And make thyself a name,"
Beguiles me on to wooing
    The phantom-form of Fame.

In vain I cry "Contented
    With quiet unknown state:"
"What! sit thee still demented,
    Complacent with dull fate?

AMBITION.

Look at thy comrades round thee
 With laurels on their brow;
Examples bright surround thee,—
 Up: and be doing now."

Ah, no! in resignation,[a]
 In spirit calm and meek,
Celestial exaltation[b]
 With all my soul I seek.
For this world's admiration,
 Tested by sacred light,
Is but abomination[c]
 In pure and holy sight.

The soul that girds upon her
 Humility's fair robe,[d]
Shines with a radiant honour
 Unseen on earth's dark globe,
Whose God[e] men's eyes hath blinded
 To worship pomp and pride,
As though 'twere noble-minded
 God's glory to deride.

That glory shines transcendent
 In His meek lowly Face,
Who came enrobed resplendent
 In Gospel truth and grace;
The meek who now adore Him
 Shall His salvation see,
And they who bow before Him,
 They shall exalted be.

AMBITION.

In His right hand are treasures,[f]—
    Bright crowns of heavenly gold;
In His pure Presence pleasures
    Man's heart hath never told:
A joy imagination
    Hath never yet conceived,
By deepest inspiration
    Revealed, by faith believed.

'Tis there my soul's ambition
    Soars, and with eagle-eye
Drinks in the dazzling vision—
    Bright immortality!
My God-breathed inspiration,
    My burning thirst divine,
Forecast my exaltation,—
    Christ,[g] God, and Heaven are mine.

[a] "Come, Resignation, spirit meek,
And let me kiss thy placid cheek,
And read in thy pale eye serene
Their blessing, who by faith can wean
Their hearts from sense, and learn to love
God only, with the joys above."
    Keble: Christian Year, 6th Sunday before Easter.

[b] Luke xiv. 11.   [c] Luke xvi. 15.   [d] Proverbs xv. 33.
[e] 2 Cor. iv. 4, 6.   [f] Psalm xvi. 11. 1 Cor. ii. 9, 10. Isaiah lxiv. 4.
[g] 1 Corinthians iii. 21—23.

One Word.

"MARY!"   "RABBONI!"

JOHN XX. 16.

ONE thrilling word! 'twas all that Jesus said,
And weeping Mary raised and turned her head;
That gentle sound stole through her inmost soul
A wondrous spell that could her grief controul;
'Twas heard, and echoed through her bursting heart,
Bidding her anguish cease, her woe depart;
While joy and wonder, mingling, took their place,
And mingling tears and smiles suffused her face:
One word—'twas all the weeper could reply,
So deep, so earnest, was her ecstacy!—
"Rabboni!"—'twas enough, her Saviour heard:
Love had rekindled love by magic of one word!

The Three Marys.

LUKE I. 26—38. JOHN XII. 3; XX. 1.—18.

ARY! thrice-favoured name
    Mentioned in sacred story,
Virgin—to whom the angel came
    Robed in resplendent glory.

Mary—who wiped the feet,
    With her luxuriant tresses,
Of Jesus, as He sat at meat,
    And bathed them with caresses.

Poor Mary Magdalene!
    Her mournful vigil keeping,
Who, early at the tomb, was seen
    In lonely sorrow weeping.

O sweet, thrice-honoured Name!
    Embalmed in sacred story,
Enriched with more than monarch's fame,
    Or earthly hero's glory!

The Ministry of Angels.

HEBREWS I. 14.

"Are they not all ministering spirits, sent forth to minister for them who shall be heirs of salvation."

EIRS of Salvation! bright angels attending,
    Minist'ring spirits sent forth from on high,
    Guiding, encamping around,ª and defending,
    By day and by night ever hovering nigh.

Chariots and horses of fire ᵇ surround us,
    Veiled though they be from our sin-clouded sight,—
Yet still ascending, descending around us,
    As the bright dream ᶜ of the ladder of light.

What though fell powers of darkness ᵈ assailing,
    Foul wicked spirits with hell-furnished might,
Wrestling in prayer, with Jehovah prevailing,
    We shall as Princes of God ᵉ win the fight.

Heirs of Salvation and glory immortal!
    Lift up your heads: bright Redemption draws nigh;
Soon shall fly open the heavenly portal,
    Soon shall return our loved King from on high.

THE MINISTRY OF ANGELS.

Princes and powers of darkness, whose legions
    Long have disturbed and disputed His sway,
Hurled into flaming unquenchable regions,
    Shall flee from His presence in dire dismay.

Lift up your heads, ye sealed Heirs of Salvation!
    See the Great Prince coming forth in His might;
Ye shall inherit the fair new creation,
    Citizen saints of the Kingdom of Light.

[a] Psalm xxxiv. 7.   [b] 2 Kings vi. 16, 17.   [c] Genesis xxxiii. 12.
    [d] Ephesians vi. 12.   [e] Genesis xxxii. 26, 27.

A Hymn.

PIRIT of Truth, inspire my prayer!
Help me on God to cast my care;
Boldly t' approach the throne of grace,
To seek His favour and His face.

Teach me to love the Lord my God,
To tread the path my Saviour trod,
My neighbour as myself to love,
And fix my thoughts on things above.

Restore my soul; and oh! make plain
Thy way, that I ne'er swerve again
To right or left, but onward go
Where streams of peace and wisdom flow.

Make me lie down midst tender grass,
Where roaring lion may not pass;
Oh! lead me onward, to that home
Where Christ's own sheep for ever roam:

Go in and out, and pasture find
Of sweetest, most celestial kind;
Bask in the light,—serenely rest
'Neath God's own glory, ever blest!

Eye hath not seen.

"Eye hath not seen, nor ear heard."

1 Cor. ii. 9, 10.

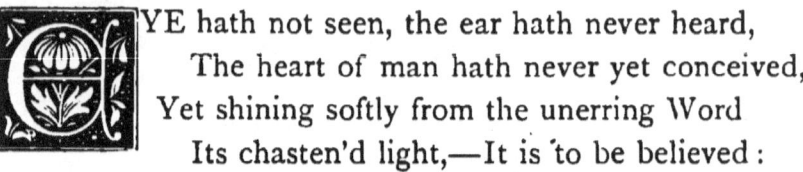YE hath not seen, the ear hath never heard,
    The heart of man hath never yet conceived,
Yet shining softly from the unerring Word
    Its chasten'd light,—It is 'to be believed :

That there are pleasures, joys for evermore,
    At the right hand of God, enthron'd above ;
Rivers !—a boundless ocean without shore,
    Of love Divine,—unfathomable love !

Glorious Liberty.

"The freedom which the Liberator of all men, JESUS CHRIST, has purchased for us with His own blood."—*Jus Cyprium.* See "Elements of Instruction on the Church," by Christopher Wordsworth, D.D., pp. 63—65.

REAT Liberator of the human race!
    My King! to Thee I dedicate my song;
Saviour! to Thee and Thy redeeming grace
    All nations, kindreds of mankind, belong.

Thy Word—the Magna Charta of mankind!—[a]
    Thy truth alone can set the conscience free,
Emancipate the sin-enthrallèd mind,
    And bid the god-of-this-world-blinded see.

O Breath! Great Spirit of the living God!
    Bid the "dead bones" arise, and live and move;
Apply to all mankind the sprinkled blood;
    All nations Thy regeneration prove.

Pour out Thy Spirit, God! upon all flesh,
    Let all the earth Thy great salvation see;
Creation's weariness and groans refresh,
    And set its sin-imprisoned serfdom free.

GLORIOUS LIBERTY.

The knowledge of the glory of the Lord
   Cover the earth as waters fill the sea ;
More than primeval peace and bliss restored
   The paradise of God regainèd be.

The year of blest redemption and release—
   Creation's Jubilee—be ushered in ;
The Thousand Years of Righteousness and Peace,
   And sealed the doom of Satan, death, and sin.

The Father, Son, and Spirit—One TRUE GOD!
   By all acknowledged, worshipped, and ador'd,
The paths of Love and Light by all be trod,
   And Jesus reign supreme—JEHOVAH, LORD!

---

[a] Some one has finely called the Bible "the Magna Charta of the human race." In an admirable little pamphlet, "Historical Associations of the English Bible," by J. W. Morris, F.L.S.—(Longmans and Co., Paternoster Row)—I find this instructive statement :—"The author of Magna Charta was a great student of Scripture. . . . . . . The Bible was his favourite study. . . . Happy has it been for us that such men cradled liberty."—(p. 15.]

"Jehobah Nissi."

PSALM LX. 4; XX. 5.

"Thou hast given a banner to them that fear Thee, that it may be displayed because of the truth."
"In the name of God we will set up our banners."

UNFURL the banner of the Cross,
    Lift up the standard high,
Count all things but as worthless dross:
    "Redemption draweth nigh."

The cause of meekness, truth, and love,
    Of justice and of right
Shall prosper, aided from above,
    Christ's majesty and might.

Bravely the banner be display'd,
    Waved high the flag of life,
No heart be moved, distressed, dismay'd,
    Though deadly be the strife.

Our King Himself hath fought and won,
    And now He reigns supreme;
That King is God's own glorious Son—
    The heavenly harpers' theme.

JEHOVAH NISSI.

'Tis Jesus Christ, the brave God-Man!
    Heaven and earth's true King;
He nobly to our rescue ran,—
    Of Him I boast, I sing.

The Lord's own Christ, "the Son of God!"
    And blessed Mary's son,—
He only hath the wine-press trod,
    Salvation He hath won.

The Lamb of God! "the Son of Man,"
    Despised, reject of men;
In God's great Book the tale I scan,
    And trace the golden vein.

Prophets of old, in "sayings dark,"
    Lay the foundation deep;
And in this everlasting ark
    The saints securely sleep.

Apostles swell the glorious strain,
    And to the dazzling light
They point, with keener gaze again
    Direct the yearning sight:

To His exalted matchless fame—
    His majesty and love,
His wondrous beauty, noble Name,
    Joy of the saints above.

JEHOVAH NISSI.

Aloft our banners, comrades, raise,
   And as we march along
We'll shout, and swell Jehovah's praise,
   And sing the Lamb's own song.

[1] Jeremiah x. 10.

[The writer trusts that nothing in the above verses will be construed into anything of a *carnal* and earthly character, such as the clerical processions with banners emblazoned with *Deis* or *Madonnas* or such like meretricious and idolatrous displays, patronized, alas! and participated in by an unhappy bishop of our Reformed Protestant Church. JEHOVAH NISSI Himself forbid such childish perversion of spiritual Truth !]

A Spiritual Battle Song, for a Good Soldier of Jesus Christ.

2 TIMOTHY II. 3.   EPHESIANS VI. 10—17.

REAT Captain of salvation's host!
    By suffering perfect made;
I sing Thy praises, shout, and boast,
    And wave my glittering blade.

Thy righteousness, my strong cuirass,
    Both breast and back protects,
My helmet, bright as polished brass,
    Salvation's light reflects.

The proven, precious, golden shield
    To meet th' oppressor's dart;
The keen two-edgèd sword to wield
    With Christ-like skill and art.

Thus clad in armour of my God
    On left hand and on right,
I tread the field brave saints have trod,
    Strong in my Captain's might.

A SPIRITUAL BATTLE SONG.

Strong to advance, and strong to stand
   In phalanx firm and true,
Christ's soldiers move at His command,
   Their heav'n-ward pathway hew.

Though legions of Satanic foes
   Their fiery darts discharge,
In vain their brazen front oppose
   When Christ's trained cohorts charge.

Hark! through the azure welkin rings
   Th' angelic roundelay,
The news the heavenly herald brings,—
   The King hath gained the day.[b]

The foe, with broken ranks, hath fled
   In dismal blank dismay;
The saints with Christ have fought and bled,
   And gained the glorious day.

And now they swell th' immortal song,
   And shout their Captain's name;
The King to whom alone belong
   Salvation, glory, fame!

[a] Hebrews ii. 10.   [b] Rev. xvii. 14; xix. 11, 21.

The Reconciling Tree.

GALATIANS IV. 14.

" God forbid that I should glory, save in the cross of our Lord Jesus Christ."

SING the glory of the Cross,
    The Name of Him who died,
Count all thing but as dung and dross
    For Jesus crucified.

Herein I make my boast and songs,
    And magnify the Name;
To this grand theme alone belongs
    A time-defying fame.

O God forbid that I should boast
    Save in that wondrous Tree,[1]
On which my God gave up the ghost,
    From death to set me free.

O God forbid that I should sing
    Of aught save Jesu's Name;
My crucified and risen King,
    His Kingdom, Crown, and Fame.

THE RECONCILING TREE.

The just, the holy Prince of life,
    By Jew and Gentile slain,
"JESUS OF NAZARETH!" our strife
    Hath rent and torn in twain.

Now Gentile, Jew,—both bond and free
    Are one in Gospel grace:
O bless the Reconciling Tree,[b]
    Whose boughs the world embrace.

O bless our Father and our God!
    The Spirit's praises sing:
Bless David's Stem and Root and Rod—
    Christ Jesus! Saviour-King!

[a] "For blessed is the wood whereby righteousness cometh." (Wisdom xiv. 7.) Is not that the Cross.

    [b] "If but one leaf she may from thee
        Win of the Reconciling Tree."
                Christian Year, 5th Sunday after Easter.

The Armies in Heaven.

REVELATION XIX. 11—21.

THERE are " chariots and horses of fire,"
    And armies arrayed for the fight,
The Lord marcheth forth in His ire,
    In the glory and strength of His might;
The trumpets in heaven are sounding,
    Th' Archangel the signal hath blown,
There are thousands of thousands[a] surrounding
    The King on His fiery throne.

There are wonders and signs in the heaven,
    Grand thund'rings and lightnings on high,
Earth's foundations asunder are riven,
    And is uttered Creation's last cry;
Rolled away is the curtain of azure,
    And tempests and whirlwinds are tame
To the breath of the Great King's displeasure,
    Which kindleth the world in its flame.

Encircled in dazzling glory,
    With glittering diadems crown'd,
In a vesture with blood red and gory,
    The Great King on clouds is enthron'd;

THE ARMIES IN HEAVEN.

A sword, in its keenness stupendous,
   Is flashing and waving around,
Like the blaze of a furnace tremendous,
   With more than a hurricane's sound.

On horses that rival in whiteness
   Stern winter's keen blast-driven snow,
In armour whose sheen in its brightness
   Eclipseth the noon-day sun's glow;
Their helmets as lightning's flash gleaming,
   Like thunders their clarions peal,—
Aloft heaven's banners are streaming,
   As the legions in battle-form wheel.

" Principalities, now, and dominions,"
   The powers of darkness and hell,
With their myriads of once haughty minions,
   Most quickly abandon their spell;
The Usurper shall now be unseated,
   From the throne of his tyranny hurl'd,
And the armies o'erthrown and defeated
   Of the Ruler and Prince of this world.

In vain do their forces assemble,
   In vain do their leaders harangue,
From vanguard to rear one deep tremble
   Pervades the disorganized gang;
Undisciplined, wild, and disorder'd,
   They shall quickly be put to the rout,
As the armies of Heaven move forward
   And advance with a terrible shout!

THE ARMIES IN HEAVEN.

Now commenceth the carnage and slaughter:
   Heaven's armies o'erwhelmingly charge,—
In torrents from every quarter
   Their thunderbolts fatal discharge:
On the right hand and left wide deploying,
   They enclose them from vanguard to rear;
Hell's host they are routing, destroying,
   Panic-paralyzed, palsied with fear.

Their leaders deserted, forsaken,—
   " The remnant are slain with the sword,"—
By the victors triumphant are taken,
   And laid at the feet of their Lord;
They are cast in the ocean that burneth
   With fire that never may die,
And the Conqueror victorious returneth
   'Mid shouts that might loosen the sky.

     *   *   *   *   *

Once again Heaven's trumpets are sounding:
   Salvation's blest peal now is blown,
And thousands again are surrounding
   The King on His glorious throne;
Saints, seraphs, and angels are singing
   The song of the Lamb that was slain,—
Heaven's vault in deep harmony ringing,
   Re-echoes their anthems again!

    [a] Psalm lxviii. 17.   Daniel vii. 10.   Revelation v. 11.

Honourable Marriage.

"But still I was enthralled with the love of woman; nor did the Apostle *forbid me to marry.*"—*Confessions of St. Augustine*, Book viii., paragraph 2, page 134; translated by Rev. E. B. Pusey, D.D.

"ENTHRALLED with woman's love,"—ah, fatal snare!
Inordinate affection's thrall beware;
Since God's own saints and mighty men of old [a]
Have been entangled in the silken fold.

Beauty is vain, deceitful favour smiles,[b]
Or dark or soft-eyed witchery beguiles:
In Delia's lap the strong man lays his head,
And Manhood, Vigour, Honour, Faith are fled.

But Gospel-grace hath now made all things new,
Man may at Wisdom's fount his strength renew: [c]
See every good and perfect gift of love
Descending from the King's own hand above.

That which "the carnal mind" once deified,—
Fair woman's love,—is sweetly sanctified;
Becomes, when sprinkled with the holy blood,
Both pure and meet for dear domestic food.[d]

HONOURABLE MARRIAGE.

Man from the dust th' Almighty Father made,
And whiles in wondering dream and slumber laid,
Took from the throbbing heart's pulsating side
The mystic bone, and formed a living bride.

Lo! when he wakes, a wondrous form and face
Glowing with perfect beauty, joy, and grace :
"Woman! Thou'rt taken from my side and heart,
My truer, purer, softer, gentler part."

Monastic mockery hath passed away
Before the freedom of "the perfect Day,"
All priest-imposed restrictions, self-willed vows
Christ's liberty ignores and disallows.

Stone walls do not a sanctuary make
Where th' imprisoned soul its thirst may slake ;
The Truth alone can set the spirit free :—
That twain are one all Scripture doth agree.[e]

When mediæval darkness veiled the mind
And Romish rubbish manacled mankind,
"The solitary monk who shook the world"[f]
The flag of God's revealèd Truth unfurl'd.

Whom God hath joined let no man put asunder,
Nor priest nor pope, with sacer*dotish* thunder;
Incontinent celibacy corrodes
The conscience, and the flesh to madness goads.

HONOURABLE MARRIAGE.

Rome, by her false, abortive, foul miscarriage,
Forbidding fair and *honourable marriage,*[g]
Brands her own brow with mystic brazen name,
Heralds her own enormous monstrous shame.[h]

Let Bishop, Presbyter, and Layman wed:[i]
'Tis undefiled and chaste the marriage-bed;
God's truth and love—the Lamb's own chosen Bride,
His spotless Church—the sacred knot have tied.

[a] "And it came to pass ... that the sons of God saw the daughters of men that they were fair." (Genesis vi.) "Many strong men have been slain by her." (Proverbs vii. 26.)

[b] Proverbs xxxi. 29. [c] Isaiah xl. 28—31. James i. 17.

[d] "A creature not too pure nor good
For human nature's daily food."
Wordsworth.

[e] Genesis ii. 24. Matthew xix. 3—6.

[f] "The solitary monk who shook the world."—*R. Montgommery.* It was in the monastery at Erfurt that Luther found the copy of the Scriptures, the searching of which was the means—in the power of the Spirit of Truth—that led him out of Rome's thraldom and darkness into the liberty of a child of God. When he married the fair Catherine, the priests and monks raised a howl of denunciation against what they were pleased to call so sacrilegious an union, exclaiming "that the issue of such a marriage must be 'Antichrist.'" Erasmus sarcastically retorted "that if from the union of monk and nun such was the monstrous issue, there must be many Antichrists already in the world." I am delighted to see by an account from Italy, that "five nuns (comparatively young girls) have just escaped from the convent of the *Good Shepherd.*" Why HE was expressly "anointed to proclaim *liberty to the captives: the opening of the prison* to them that are bound."—Isaiah lxi. 1—3. Luke iv. 18—20.

[g] 1 Timothy iv. 3. Hebrews xiii. 4. [h] Revelation xvii. 5.

[i] 1 Timothy iii. 2—12.

"Christ our Life."

COLOSSIANS III. 1—4.

IN vain I feed on friendship,
    And pine for woman's love,
These are but choking husks at best,
    But thorns and briars prove:
My soul must feed on Christ,
    Without His love I die;
On wings of faith and hope and prayer,
    To God in Christ I fly.

"The Blood of Jesus Christ."

1 PETER I. 18—20.   1 JOHN I. 7.   EPHESIANS II. 11—22.

I SING the priceless blood of Christ
    That cleanseth man from sin,
The cost at which my soul was pric'd,
    Which God resolved to win.

'Twas not with gold and silver dust,
    'Twas not with this world's dross,—
Into God's side the spear was thrust,
    In Christ upon the Cross.

God was in Christ to reconcile—
    Christ was the Lamb that bled;—
That which my soul did once defile
    Is now destroyed and dead.

O Spotless and unblemished Lamb
    O priceless, precious blood!
In Jesus now I righteous am,
    Pure, holy, just, and good.

THE BLOOD OF JESUS CHRIST.

Blest Lamb! before the worlds ordained
    In these our times revealed;
The mystery is now explained
    For ages long concealed.

Both Jew and Gentile now are one,
    Are one who once were twain;
The miracle by Christ was done,
    The Lamb who once was slain.

Come Gentile, Jew! come Bond and Free!
    One purchased ransomed race;
Embrace "the Reconciling Tree,"
    The glorious Gospel-grace!

The Lord my Salvation.

EXODUS XV. 2.   ISAIAH XII. 2.   PSALM CXVIII. 14.

"Behold God is my salvation; I will trust and not be afraid; for the Lord Jehovah is my strength and song; He also is become my salvation."

THE Lord is my strength : in His name I defy
    The foes that would trouble and harass my soul,
And strong in His help and His grace from on high
    My fears and temptations I quell and control.

The Lord is my song ; and my soul shall rejoice,
    While grateful thanksgivings and glad hymns of praise
Shall flow from my heart and resound from my voice,
    As daily a new Ebenezer I raise.

And now is become my salvation the Lord,
    To Whom alone blessing and honour belong ;
His Name is my shield, and His Truth is my sword—
    JEHOVAH—my strength, my salvation, my song!

A Protestant Layman's Catholic Confession.

JEREMIAH XVII. 9.

"*Deceitful above all things and desperately wicked.*"

GREAT God! I dare not tell to man—
  Thine eye alone the depth can scan
    Of all my dark depravity;
  But O, dear Lord, to Thee I *dare*
  Tell all; for, lo, I read it *there*—
    The blood-red scroll on Calvary!

  My Father! as I look again
  'Tis gone: the dark and crimson stain
    Now shines as white as virgin snow;
  In lieu of sin, and death, and shame,
  I read a sweet and gracious name,
    Brighter than sun's meridian glow.

  My Father, Saviour, Teacher,—GOD!
  I dip my pen in Jesu's blood,
    So costly, precious, pure, divine.
  I write my own new,[a] living name—
  No more a child of wrath and shame—
    Great God!—a child, a son of Thine!

[a] Romans viii. 14—17. Galatians iv. 7. Revelation ii. 17; iii. 12.

"Awake, awake, put on strength, O arm of the Lord!"

ISAIAH LI. 9; LII. 1, 2.   PSALM XLV. 3, 4, 6.

AWAKE! O arm of God, awake!
    Put on victorious strength;
  O Israël, arise! retake
    Thy long-lost land at length.

Awake! Jerusalem, awake!
    Lift up thy weeping eyes;
Thy dust-stained garments, Zion, shake!
    In light and beauty rise.

Command deliverances, Lord!
    Old Jacob's God and King!
By Thine own arm, and hand, and sword,
    Thine own salvation bring.

Gird on Thy sword upon Thy thigh,
    In majesty and might;
Ride prosperously forth, Most High!
    In meekness, truth, and right.

AWAKE, AWAKE, PUT ON STRENGTH.

For ever is Thy throne, O God !
   Thy kingdom over all ;
Its sceptre is of truth the rod
   'Neath which Thy foes must fall.

The heathen and all nations soon
   Must own Thy sovereign sway ;
Thine enemies be overthrown—
   The wicked swept away.

Thou only shalt exalted be,
   Praised, honoured, and ador'd ;
" All flesh," and all the earth, shall see
   " The Glory of the Lord ! "

A Protestant Ballad of the Nineteenth Century.

ISAIAH XXI. 8—12.   HABAKKUK II. 1.

HARK! soldiers of the Cross of Christ! Hark! hark ye to the call!
From sentinel on battlement, from watchman on the wall:
The foe is stealing up the vale, right stealthily they come,
As craftily they move along to sound of muffled drum.*

Soldiers of Jesus Christ, arise! Gird quick your armour on!
Be staunch and true, and steadfast stand the Rock of truth upon;
Bold be your hearts, and firm your hands, "Quit ye like men: be strong!"
The battle may rage hot and fierce, the conflict may be long.

Arouse! arouse from revelling, from slumber, and from sleep;
Away ye to the ramparts, and your posts with courage keep!
Up drawbridge,—down portcullis! Ho! ye warders, have a care!
The foe come stealing up the vale, right stealthily: beware!

Brave comrades of the Cross of Christ! look well unto your
  gear,
Your helmets and your corselets all be polished bright and
  clear :
Your greaves and gauntlets, coats of mail, your tried and
  proven shield ;
Look that your two-edged swords be keen, and manfully
  them wield.

Our Captain's eye is over us, beholding from above,
And o'er our ranks there floateth fair His banner broad of
  love !
Be not as fools who beat the air : fight the good fight of faith,
Our Captain is our God and Guide, aye, even unto death.

Salvation's[b] burnished helmet plant ye firm upon your brows,
Buckle ye on the breast-plate bright, with righteousness that
  glows ;
Bind on the coat of mail of truth ;—Faith in the truth our
  shield ;
The two-edged sword—the Word of God—in Christ's own
  strength we'll wield.

The Gospel-greaves of love and peace bind firm upon your
  feet,
In Christ, our Captain-God, stand fast, brave, steadfast, calm,
  complete ;
Let thousands and ten thousands of our present foes assail,
Nor they, nor yet " the gates of hell," against us shall pre
  vail.

THE NINETEENTH CENTURY.

Brave comrades of the Cross of Christ! though hardness we endure,
Our Captain is our strength and shield, His faithfulness is sure :
His eye still watches over us, beholding from above,
While o'er our serried ranks still floats His banner bright of love !

[a] Tractarian Jesuitism.   [b] Ephesians vi. 10—18.

"He is the Rock."

PSALM XVIII. 31, 46.　DEUTERONOMY XXXII. 31;
XXXIII. 29.　PSALM LXII. 2, 6, 7.　1 CORINTHIANS X. 4.
2 SAMUEL XXII. 32, 47.

" Who is God save the Lord? and who is a Rock save our God?"
" The Lord liveth; and blessed be my Rock; and exalted be the God of the Rock of my Salvation."

WHO is God, save Christ the Lord?
　　Who is a Rock, save Christ our God?
Blest Israel's help, and shield and sword,
　　As through their wilderness they trod.

" That Rock was Christ "—the smitten Rock,—
　　They drank the living streams that flowed,—
Cloud-pillar! shelt'ring all His flock,
　　By night a fiery safeguard glowed.

So David's Son, and David's Lord,
　　Was David's only Rock and God!
His gracious Shepherd to afford
　　The comfort of His staff and rod.

HE IS THE ROCK.

His sun, salvation, shield and song,
   Strength, light, and glory, tower of grace!
None like Him all the gods among,—
   He sang the glories of His face.

His kingdom, sceptre, crown, and throne,
   Might, honour, majesty, and love!
Great Prophet, Priest, Prince, King alone
   Of earth below, of heaven above.

And still the saints repeat the song,
   And still recount the wondrous theme;
Honours divine to them belong,
   To hymn th' exalted One, Supreme!

Jehovah is our strength and song,
   Salvation's everlasting Rock,
To Christ—the Shepherd, Lamb,—belong
   Gentile and Jew, in one blest flock.

The Worldling's rock is shadow, sand,—
   Gold, science, pleasure, phantom-fame;
The Rock we boast, on which we stand,
   Jehovah-Jesu's saving Name!

No other may withstand the shock,
   When heaven and earth alike shall shake,
When kingdoms to their centre rock,
   And universal powers quake.

HE IS THE ROCK.

Come! heroes, sages, princes, kings!
    In east and west, in north and south;
Lo! Zion's God salvation brings,
    Let His high praises fill your mouth.

Youths, maidens, fathers, swell the song,
    Shout, shout the One exalted Name!
Hosannas loud, ye lisping throng,
    Let Zion's children ring the fame!

Hark! hark! the rapture-thrilling strain,—
    He comes! He comes! uplift ye gates!
The King of Glory comes to reign,
    While the fair Bride expectant waits.

Who is this King of Glory! Who?
    The Lord of Hosts! the Great, the Strong!
The Faithful, Righteous, Just, and True,
    To Whom both heaven and earth belong.

Lo! every knee adoring bends;
    Hark! every tongue resounds the claim,
From heaven, earth, hell, the shout ascends:
    JESUS is LORD! all, all proclaim.

Yes! He is LORD! the Saviour-King!
    Omega, Alpha, First and Last!
The Name, the Man, the God I sing,
    Light of the future, present, past.

HE IS THE ROCK.

O bless the Father of our Lord!
   O bless the Gospel-grace and fame;
O bless the Spirit, and accord
   High glory unto Jesu's Name!

Psalm xlv. 2. 2 Cor. vi. 6. Psalm lxxxvi. 8; lxxxix. 6, 8; cx. and cxlv. Exodus xv. 2. Psalm cxviii. 14. Isaiah xii. 2. Acts iv. 12. Psalm cxlviii. 11, 12, 13; cxlix. 2, 6, 9. Philippians ii. 9, 10, 11. Revelation xxi. 6; xxii. 13.

The Harps of God.

"Bring me a minstrel. And it came to pass when the minstrel played, that the hand of the Lord came upon him."

2 Kings iii. 15.

"And I heard a voice from heaven, as the voice of many waters, and as the voice of a great thunder: and I heard the voice of harpers harping with their harps." "Having the harps of God. And they sing the song of Moses the servant of God, and the song of the Lamb."

Revelation xiv. 2; xv. 2.

"BRING me a minstrel!" Strike the harps of heaven!
"O give me music"—Music from above!
Sing me of what my God to man hath given
Of glory, in the Son of His dear love.

The hand, the Spirit of the Lord descend,—
Inspire and fill and energize my soul;
The holy fire with my rapt spirit blend,
Expand, inflame, and yet my muse control.

The music of celestial choirs and spheres!
Anthems of angels! Heavenly harpers' theme!
The loved Apostle's rapture, joy and tears,—
Th' Apocalyptic vision, trance and dream.

THE HARPS OF GOD.

Rich melody Divine! Seraphic strain!
  The soul-entrancing music,—"Harps of God!"
The song of Moses and the Lamb once slain,
  Who has redeemed us with His precious blood.

"O Great and marvellous Thy works, Lord God!
  Almighty King of ages, nations, saints!
O just and true Thy ways:"—"for they their blood [b]
  Have shed:" and Thou hast heard their vengeance-
    plaints.[c]

Who shall not fear Thee? Glorify Thy Name?
  Thou *only* holy art,—the only Lord!
All nations shall Thy majesty proclaim,—
  Fame, honour, glory, praise, to Thee accord.

Sing—The Lord God omnipotent now reigns!
  Sing—Alleluia! He hath judged the whore,—[d]
The harlot with her thousand scarlet stains—
  Whose smoke ascendeth up for evermore.

O music as of many waters, voices!
  Deep thunder-diapason, song of songs!
The universal choir of heaven rejoices,—
  "Salvation unto God, and to the Lamb belongs!"[e]

[a] Revelation v. 4, 5.   [b] Revelation xvi. 5, 6.   [c] Revelation vi. 10, 11.
     [d] Revelation xix. 1—6.   [e] Revelation vii. 10.

"The Church of God."

ACTS XX. 28.

"And I believe one Catholic and Apostolic Church."
Nicene Creed.

HIGH, LOW, BROAD, FREE.

Matthew xxviii. 18—20.   Mark xvi. 15—20.   Ephesians ii. 18—22.
Isaiah xxviii. 16.   Psalm cxviii. 22.   1 Corinthians iii. 11.
1 Peter ii. 4—10.

THE Church of GOD is One,
   High as the heavens above,—
Low as our deeply-fallen state,—
   Free as GOD's boundless love.

Broad as from East to West,
   Where oceans freely roll;
She would embrace the human race,—
   Mankind from Pole to Pole.

For every age and clime,
   For every tribe of man,
For every creature Gospel-grace—
   The Proclamation ran.

THE CHURCH OF GOD.

Built on the One True Rock,
   Apostles, Prophets found,—
The Christ of God, Whose voice the flock
   Hear, and accept the sound.

One grand chief Corner-Stone
   By God the Father laid,
In Jesus Christ Himself, through Whom
   The Spirit was display'd.

Each saint a "living-stone"
   On that One Living Rock!
Gentile or Jew, or Bond or Free,[a]
   One living, loving flock.

Our Shepherd, Bishop, HE,
   Our Prophet, Priest, and King!
All ye who love Him, peace with ye:[b]
   Let us His praises sing.

[a] Colossians iii. 11.   1 Peter ii. 3—10.
[b] 1 Peter ii. 25.   Ephesians vi. 23, 24.

A Lutheran Epigram.

A WORM that lived upon a Rock [a]
    Who overturn'd and shook the world,
By whom, with more than earthquake shock,
    A tyrant from his throne was hurl'd.

[a] "And that Rock was Christ."—1 Cor. x. 4.

A Romish Epigram.

IF ever Rome shall rule the roast,
    Then roasting will become the rule;
Brave Freedom may give up the ghost,
    Priest Superstition play the fool.

Vox Populi.

JOHN VI. 15; XIX. 14, 15.

TO-DAY, they'll crown Him, King!—Anon, they cry,
"Away with Him! Away to crucify!"

A Sinner Saved by Grace.

1 CORINTHIANS XV. 10.

" By the grace of God, I am what I am."

SINNER saved by grace!
  My matins, even-song,
I'll troll it forth from place to place,
  My pilgrim path along.

" Dear blood, redeeming grace!"[a]
  Inspire my gladsome lays,
The light of God in Jesu's face,[b]
  I'll sing, and pen, and praise.

A sinner saved by grace!
  No work, no merit mine,
I would myself in dust abase,
  Exalt the love divine:

The " everlasting love "[c]
  Of God in Christ to man,
The theme of angel-song above,
  Salvation's matchless plan.

A SINNER SAVED BY GRACE.

Though "chief of sinners" I,
  Yet would I not despair,
But meekly to the cross draw nigh,
  And read my pardon there.

Exulting in the name,
  I would proclaim the story,
Extolling sovereign grace's fame,
  JEHOVAH'S TRIUNE GLORY!

ᵃ Whatever be the thoughts of men of these things; free grace and dear blood will ever be the stay of the redeemed on earth, and the everlasting song of the glorified in heaven.—*Traill's Sermon on the Throne of Grace.*

ᵇ 2 Corinthians iv. 6.   ᶜ Jeremiah xxxi. 3.   Revelation v. 9—14.

www.ingramcontent.com/pod-product-compliance
Lightning Source LLC
Chambersburg PA
CBHW032142160426
43197CB00008B/754